Th

The Gameshooter's Pocket Guide has ...
latest essentials of gameshooting. It is a compact, encyc... :
compendium of facts, rules, shooting etiquette and lore for the use
of both novices and seasoned gameshooters.

Chapters cover safety, legal requirements, choice of gun
and equipment, dress, etiquette, game seasons, dogs, teaching a
novice, rules for beginners, rough-shooting and many other details
that all gameshooters might need to know. Appendices list useful
addresses of representative organisations and shooting schools.
Information on shooting seasons, shot sizes and essential safety
points in the field are presented in tabular form for easy reference.

Gameshooting continues to attract a growing following,
making it all the more important that gameshooting enthusiasts
learn and adhere to the fundamental rules of field safety and
behaviour. This guide will serve as an ideal companion for
gameshooters at all levels, regardless of nationality, wishing to
avoid being a danger and embarrassment in the shooting field.

The Author

Michael Brook is a retired cavalry officer whose limited career
prospects tended to take second place to recreational activities,
not least fieldsports and, in particular, gameshooting. He was
introduced to shooting, as a small boy, by his grandfather. He lives
in North Yorkshire with his wife, Bridget. He is keen to promote
and preserve the true spirit of gameshooting.

GAMESHOOTER'S
Pocket Guide

Michael Brook

Line drawings by
Mark Conroy

Merlin Unwin Books

This edition published by Merlin Unwin Books Ltd, 2014
Originally published by B.T. Batsford Ltd, 1990

Merlin Unwin Books Ltd
Palmers House, 7 Corve Street
Ludlow, Shropshire SY8 1DB

www.merlinunwin.co.uk

ISBN 978-1-906122-59-1

Designed and set in Calibri by Merlin Unwin
Printed and bound by Short Run Press Ltd, Exeter.

For Nugget:
the most loving, competent and human
dog I have ever known and owned

CONTENTS

ACKNOWLEDGEMENTS

Obviously, I could not have written this book without experience of gameshooting. Much of my experience has been gained through the generosity of those who have invited me to shoot over the years. I could name all of my hosts. I rather think, though, that few, if any, would thank me for doing so. Nevertheless, I would like to express my sincere gratitude to them all.

From BASC I would like to thank Jeffrey Olstead, Bill Harriman and Glynn Evans. I am deeply indebted also to David Frost, author of *Sporting Shooting and the Law*, for his freely given and extraordinarily prompt advice on the current law relating to gun ownership and gameshooting.

Mark Conroy, whose evocative illustrations adorn each chapter, has been a great source of inspiration over the years, with his encyclopaedic knowledge of nature, especially matters ornithological and piscatorial. Indeed, when I was faced with a bleak stint abroad where I knew that the shooting opportunities were distinctly unsporting and therefore to be avoided on principle, Mark gave me a crash course in fly-fishing. While I enjoy my fishing, I rate myself somewhat immodestly as possibly one of the world's most useless fishermen; Mark is precisely the opposite.

I always enjoy a day's shooting immeasurably more if accompanied by Bridget my wife. It is her support, regardless of the standard of my marksmanship on a given day, that I value most and which deserves better acknowledgement than I can give here.

Finally I must say what a joy it has been working with Karen McCall of Merlin Unwin Books. She has been unfailingly courteous, efficient, patient and wise with her suggestions and amendments, for which I am deeply grateful.

INTRODUCTION

It is gratifying to realise that little has changed in the gameshooting world since I wrote the first edition of *The Gameshooter's Pocket Guide* and that the book has stood the test of time with only one main exception, that of clothing. There have been dramatic changes and developments in textiles and materials in recent years. It is now possible to buy easily-affordable, genuinely breathable but waterproof, strong, warm, light and machine-washable coats, specifically designed for the gameshooter. The critical advantage of such garments is that they offer the wearer extremely good protection against the elements, without hindering his or her ability to shoot safely and comfortably, whereas previously some clothing could be a potentially dangerous hindrance. In passing, I should add also that gameshooting, in general, has become much better regulated from within.

The inspiration for this book came from the fact that I was an involuntary target twice on formal shoots, in the same season. Such experience tends to affect one's enjoyment and to focus one's mind. Having seen other dangerous incidents over the years, I felt that there was a need for a book about shooting safety and etiquette.

The purposes of this book, therefore, are twofold. First, to provide an *aide-memoire* for an experienced shot training a child; typically, a father teaching his son. Secondly, it is aimed at the adult novice who receives an invitation to shoot or merely decides to take up gameshooting for whatever reason.

The child is fortunate in that he can take his time and only be allowed to shoot once a third party (usually his father) decides that he is safe and ready to do so. It is the adult who is less fortunate and who is most likely to prove a menace to his fellows. He has to absorb a great deal of advice and theory in a very short period; theory that can only be put into context, inevitably, in the shooting field.

Shooting, like any hobby or pursuit, should be a pleasure and should never be at the expense of somebody else's well-being. While this book is about safety, it is also about good manners – in an ideal world, they are one and the same thing. Since, as already stated, we are all fallible, not least the author, it is no bad thing to revise a few sound principles occasionally; it is a very rare person who can put his hand on his heart and swear that he has never fired a dangerous shot – I know that I cannot. However safe one might think one is, it is very perilous to bask in a sea of complacency. A moment's lapse of concentration could result in anyone, however safe normally, doing something dangerous, which could risk somebody else's life. No sane person goes shooting in the hope of risking his or her life but it is terrifyingly easy to risk somebody else's life. I hope, most fervently, that this book might contribute to safety in the shooting field. I should stress at this stage, that it is rare that I return from a day's shooting without having learnt something new, not least with regard to the ways of nature, which, of course, is why gameshooting is so interesting.

It has not been my intention to describe every possible type of shoot. Thus, in Chapter 1, I describe an average, fairly informal driven shoot, which, although privately owned, would be similar if syndicated. I hope that this approach will cater for the great majority of people new to gameshooting. I urge the patient reader to read Chapter 1 and then re-read it as it has so much to offer the aspiring gameshooting apprentice, especially any notes at the bottom of each page; actually, it may even offer something of value to the experienced gameshot. Although the views expressed in this book are one man's, and based to a great extent on his experience, they are bolstered also by reference to other sources considerably wiser, more knowledgeable and experienced than the author.

There is increasing political and media pressure on gameshooting, which has led to the drawing up of a Code of Good Game Shooting Practice by a joint committee formed by the British Association for Shooting and Conservation (BASC), Countryside Alliance (CA) and the Game and Wildlife Conservation Trust (GWCT). Every element of this code is included in the relevant parts of this book.

While safety is paramount, respect for the quarry is also essential. If you do not want to eat what you shoot, unless you give it to a friend who does, then perhaps you should not be shooting game. Those on a shoot should also be mindful about not being too greedy about the number of birds shot. Misbehaviour, due to ignorance, uncertainty, or bad manners by a small minority, can bring the whole sport into disrepute and ruin it, potentially, for the majority. If this small book reduces the risk of that happening, then it will have achieved its purpose.

Michael Brook
June 2014

1

A DAY'S SHOOTING ETIQUETTE

This chapter is unlike all the other chapters in this book. While the rest contains practical advice, I open with a narrative of a typical shooting day: I hope a useful device to get my message across. For those with natural good manners it may be a useful memory-jogger but it is not a failsafe for those with limited consideration for others. Suffice it to say that rudeness is most unlikely to result in a second invitation to shoot.

'Sorry' is one word which should always be ready to hand – it costs nothing and can turn a potential disaster into a success; sometimes, that is. Successive poaching of a neighbouring Gun's birds, followed by a shrill 'Sorry!' becomes a totally threadbare excuse after only two uses.

It is remarkable, too, how reassuring an apology can be, particularly if a neighbour has shot a little too close to oneself for comfort. This sort of apology takes some courage to admit but is much appreciated. The maxim is: 'Be safe at all times', followed by: 'If in doubt, ask.'

WHAT FOLLOWS IS WHAT MIGHT HAPPEN ON A DAY'S SHOOTING, although the occasions when one might shoot grouse, duck, partridge and pheasant on the same shoot on the same day are fairly rare. While such a day might be possible in Scotland or the north of England, because of the presence of grouse, it is not exactly typical and has been contrived to make various points. Grouse will most certainly not be found on shoots in Hampshire or Sussex, for example, however grand the shoot!

1

PRELIMINARIES

'George, it's Charles Chute-Strait. I was wondering whether you could shoot at Feudal Park on 2nd November? You can? Oh, excellent. Look, old chap, it's very informal...' George knew Charles well and realised that 'informal' did not mean jeans and an old combat jacket. 'We meet at the house at 0915 hours. We'll have a go at grouse, partridge and pheasant (1) so bring plenty of cartridges. Oh, yes, and do stay for the evening flight.' George did a quick mental check-list: Charles had told him where to go and when, what to wear and a rough idea of what to expect; what else? 'Ah, Charles. Do you mind if I bring the dog or would you prefer me to leave him behind?'

'No, delighted as long as he's well-behaved. I'm sure you'd keep him tethered anyway if he wasn't too steady.'

'One last question, Charles (2). Shall I bring lunch?'

'Good point, old chap, I should have mentioned it. Liz is away so I can't provide lunch. Please bring your own, and I will provide the liquid refreshment. We gather in the old lodge for lunch, so it'll be fairly dry and comfortable. We'll look forward to seeing you'.

Note: (1) *It is one of the idiosyncrasies of gameshooting that, in most contexts, feathered game is referred to in the singular eg 'We shot pheasant and partridge today'.*

(2) *This is the stage at which you can have all your questions answered. It is rash and most impolite to turn up with, for example, a companion without first clearing it with your host. If you receive a written invitation as opposed to a verbal one, it is imperative that you reply to it without delay even if the shoot is several weeks or, possibly, months ahead.*

Charles, George remembered, always insisted that guns be carried in gun sleeves, a philosophy with which George completely agreed. Interestingly, Charles also insisted that his syndicate guns, at the start of the season, produce an up-to-date certificate from a gunsmith, declaring their guns to be safe. Charles would have liked to extend this directive to his guests but was experienced enough to know that this might not always be a practicable criterion for them to accede to. George was aware that Charles had not mentioned Fiona, his wife. He would miss her company, but decided that additional guests must obviously not be expected. At least he would have Nugget, his yellow Labrador, who was always a perfect companion.

'Why's he called Nugget?' he was often asked, to which his reply was: 'It's an easy name to bellow and he is yellow like gold.'

Arrival

George arrived at Feudal Park at 0900 hours, 15 minutes before Charles had suggested, in good time to put on his boots, jacket and other gear and to assemble his gun and equipment. His father had always said: 'Early to shoot, late to dinner, me boy; i.e. get to the shoot in good time or you might ruin your host's plans.' (3) Although he had put out everything the night before, prior to

---

Note: (3) *Late arrival could ruin a carefully planned day and also result in extra expense for the host or syndicate. A useful benchmark is to arrive 15 minutes early so that you can orientate yourself, don shooting garb, organise kit and generally relax but be very careful not to impose on your host who will be very busy at this stage. If you arrive late and flustered, inevitably it will have a bad effect on your performance and enjoyment.*

setting off he had meticulously re-checked his kit, just in case he had missed something. Although he had not done so personally, he knew people who had left their guns behind and he had forgotten the odd item, too, which tended, however trivial, to overshadow an otherwise good day. The worst thing he had done in the past was to forget his shooting coat, which was very inconvenient since it contained several necessities.

He quickly ran through the **GAMESHOOTER'S CHECK-LIST**: *jacket, money* for tips and petrol on the way home, *cap, gloves* (both wool outers and silk inners), *scarf, leggings, safety goggles* (worn as a sensible precaution when shooting driven grouse) *first aid kit, pocket-knife, pencil and paper, cartridge bag* (full), *cartridge belt* (full), *gun, gun sleeve, boots and socks, ear defenders* (both plugs and electronic ear muffs), *dog, dog whistle, dog lead, dog's waterbowl, tick twister* (an inexpensive and effective tool for removing ticks which may be prevalent on grouse moors, obtainable from a vet), *dog's water* and a few *biscuits*. What else? Ah, yes, *dog's towelling coat* (so much better than just a towel) and *torch* for the duckflight, plus *lunch and liquid refreshment*, of course. As if that was not enough, there was the last vital prop – his *stick,* which was handy for support over rough ground and for pegging the dog if no pegs were provided. Attached to the stick was his *leather protector* (*see* note on page 25).

He was not the first to arrive and quickly introduced himself to those who had arrived before him; he noticed too that another Gun had brought a guest and was assiduously introducing him to everybody (4). Another Gun had brought his 10-year-old son, who

---

Note: (4) *Do not be shy, so that people can get to know you quickly. If you are an established member of a shoot, make strangers welcome.*

was not going to shoot but shadow his father as part of his tutoring in the mores of shooting. He was pleasantly surprised to see that Charles, previously a renowned male chauvinist, had invited a lady Gun. George knew her slightly but knew her reputation as a crack-shot far better. She missed very few birds, even on an off-day and was modest with it.

He kept Nugget on the lead but gave him the chance to accustom himself to the scenery and do what most dogs like to do after a journey. Rather than risk his dog depositing an unsavoury pile at the shoot rendez-vous, George had reduced that risk by taking him for a walk before leaving home.

The Briefing

At 0915, Charles Chute-Strait gathered the Guns together and introduced the guests (5). Then he outlined the day ahead, before asking the Guns to draw for pegs. 'We number from the right and move up two places each drive.'

George listened attentively to his host, even though he was keen to chat to one of the other Guns, who was an old friend he had not seen for a while. Thus, significantly, he discovered that they would not be coming back to the cars before the end of the day. This meant taking cartridge bags and lunch on the trailer. He had forgotten lunch once and shivered with embarrassment as he recalled the humiliation he had felt at accepting his fellow Guns'

Note: (5) *The number of Guns may vary between six and twelve, eight being an average figure. Too many Guns are difficult to control and to fit comfortably around coverts, when the usual distance between Guns is about 40 yards. Sometimes, Guns may be detailed to be a walking Gun on a drive.*

charity; actually he had done rather well, but preferred not to have to repeat the experience.

As Charles finished his briefing, George went up to him and said quietly, 'Charles, what's your new keeper's name and what can we shoot?'

'Jem Morgan's his name. Good of you to ask. Bother, I should have mentioned the quarry. Shoot pheasant, partridge, grouse, snipe and woodcock. No ground game under any circumstances. Oh, and please don't shoot foxes,' Charles replied, secretly kicking himself for not having included such fundamental points in his briefing (6).

Before climbing on the trailer, George made a point of introducing himself to the keeper.

The trailer was somewhat draughty, George reflected, as they bumped up a rutted track to the first drive. Sometimes on a shoot there was no need for transport at all, sometimes Guns were moved in Land Rovers and other four-wheel drive vehicles (very smart) and sometimes they took their cars from drive to drive. It all depended on distances and the terrain to be covered.

Note: (6) *Most shoots used to have an agreement with their local hunt and, therefore, did not shoot foxes. Despite the 2004 ban on hunting, foxes tend to be shot only where no hunt could safely go. Even then, unless a fox is within a few feet, rather than yards, it should be left, since foxes are hard to kill with a shotgun and can easily be only wounded, to die an agonising, lingering death.*

THE FIRST DRIVE

They arrived at the start of the first drive, which, due to the lie of the land, George judged to be a pheasant drive. Charles escorted George to his peg which was marked by a stick with a split in the top and a number inserted in the split. 'The birds will come from that direction. Just watch out for the walking Gun who will appear to your left later on,' said Charles helpfully in a low voice before wandering off to his own peg.

On the way, Charles nudged one of the Guns who was strolling towards his peg and talking loudly to another Gun, indicating with a finger to his lips to keep quiet (7). George took his bearings and ensured that the Guns either side of him acknowledged where he was. He surveyed all the ground around him in a 360-degree arc so that he knew instinctively the danger spots, where not to shoot, where the birds might fly to, the location of any pickers-up – at the start of a drive, he made a point of indicating to pickers-up that he knew they were there - and that there were no people who should not be there (8). Having tethered Nugget, he took his gun from its sleeve, breaking it open before it was clear of the sleeve, then

---

Note: (7) *Game is easily disturbed and, if forewarned, will sit tight, thereby ruining that drive and sport for everybody else. Inevitably this also means that people's money is being wasted; therefore, noise and talking should be avoided as much as possible. This maxim applies equally if the Guns are being moved in open transport.*
(8) *There may well be pickers-up. Normally they should be well back, concealed and out of range but beware, since some tend to creep towards the Guns without you or themselves realizing it.*

checked the barrels were clear (9) and loaded it. When a whistle indicated the start of the drive, he closed the gun, checked the safety catch was on and stood with the gun held under his arm pointing at the ground, waiting for the pheasants.

Nothing happened for ages but he resisted the temptation to leave his peg to talk to his fellow Guns and refrained too from fiddling with his gun.

Suddenly a voice from the beating line cried, 'Forward!' (10) He looked ahead and saw a hen pheasant flying towards him. He started to raise his gun but, because in his estimation the bird was too low, did not fire at it. The hen was followed soon afterwards by a cock which was nearer him than the Gun on his right. He was just raising his gun when there was a bang and the bird fell dead behind him. 'Sorry, I think that should really have been yours,' said the perpetrator, almost too hastily. The same Gun then shot at a bird which was patently out of range. Unfortunately he pricked it and it flew on quite strongly, even though obviously wounded. Nugget

---

Note: (9) *The slightest blockage could cause a burst barrel when fired.* **(10)** *It is hard to dictate when to warn a neighbour of approaching quarry and it should only be done if he is going to be genuinely taken by surprise, otherwise it can be most off-putting. Also, a noisy Gun enables birds in cover to pinpoint exactly where they are and to take avoiding action accordingly; thus, it is wise to bide your time and see if regular members do it. There is a homily which says that with a 50/50 bird ie one roughly half-way between 2 Guns, one should leave it for the other Gun. Interestingly, few birds pass with neither Gun addressing them. Another convention is that it is only courteous to leave a bird crossing one's front, either obliquely or parallel, if it is flying directly at a neighbouring Gun.*

looked up at George as if to say, 'You wouldn't dream of doing such a thing, would you, Master?'

Before he could dwell on his neighbour's misdemeanours any further, George was faced with a steady stream of birds. Carefully selecting one bird at a time and always the highest and most sporting birds in his opinion, rather than flitting from target to target before firing, he shot several birds before a lull occurred. With the benefit of many years' experience, George tried to shoot his quarry in the head rather than merely aiming at the bulk of the bird in the hope of bringing it down. Nugget looked at him admiringly, wagging his tail happily and obviously proud of Master's prowess; George resisted the temptation to let Nugget off to start picking up the dead birds, although his neighbour's dog was running loose, picking up other Guns' birds. Nugget was not impressed either (11).

As the beaters hove into sight, George raised his barrels skywards to show that he had seen them and would only take high birds or birds behind. Shortly afterward, Jem Morgan blew a whistle as a signal that the drive was over and Guns should unload. George turned his barrels away from the beaters, unloaded and put his gun back in its sleeve, before releasing Nugget to retrieve his birds.

Although he enjoyed carrying his birds to the game-cart – as a manifestation of his success – he cheerfully handed over his birds

---

Note: (11) *Dogs should be kept in until the end of a drive and never released before, in order to avoid distracting the Guns, not least their owners. Loose dogs can be shot accidentally if ground game is permitted, can easily disturb the game from both the present and subsequent drives, and distract other Guns.*

to a beater who offered to carry them (12). Then, he walked back to a picker-up to direct her to a bird he thought she may not have marked (13).

As he and Nugget walked back to the trailer, they were joined by a rather tiresome individual. 'I got six that time for 16 cartridges.

Note: (12) *It is customary to let beaters carry the bag unless they are overburdened and would appreciate help - do not force the issue. Regardless of who carries the birds, game should be carried as they will be hung in the game-cart and, subsequently, in the game larder, by the head not upside down by the feet. A bird's feet are likely to carry potent germs since they are not choosy where they walk or what they tread in.*

(13) *Marking accurately where wounded birds land is essential so that pickers-up are not sent on some fruitless mission. A vague 'Oh, it's somewhere over there' is not helpful, wastes time and, fundamentally, is rude. Accurate marking comes with practice but there are simple principles that can be adopted to improve the pick-up rate. If you think you have hit a bird, do not ignore it and carry on shooting more birds, instead watch it as far as you can to see where it lands, noting any easily identifiable reference points such as trees, bushes, gates or other permanent features. This establishes a line between you and the area to be searched, which is vital and hugely increases the chances of finding that bird. Having directed the picker-up onto the line, you should then describe the area and reference points as precisely as possible.*

If there are no pickers-up and you are looking for a bird, be careful not to spend too long searching for it lest you upset your host's plans. Do make a point of telling a picker-up where you think it might be; failing that tell the keeper or your host, as soon as you can.

I reckon that makes my average for the season about 2.7 cartridges per bird.' George smiled politely at him and said something vague like, 'Really? Well done. I never dare tally up because I'm sure it would be too much of a shock.' Somehow it seemed infra dig to work out one's cartridge-to-kill ratio, and talking about it was tantamount to boasting. Besides, he never had any real idea how many cartridges he had fired and, if he did, it would probably make him give up shooting altogether.

George was about to climb aboard the trailer when Charles said, 'George, old chap, would you like to walk with the beaters this drive? It's usually good value . . . quite busy.' George duly joined the beaters and was gratified when Jem Morgan said, 'You're in the hot seat this time sir, the royal box so to speak. By the way, it's a special day today since, because of the drives we're doing, you could theoretically shoot at least eight different species. Leastways, the record's eight, won by Mr Chute-Strait's father in 1952.'

It sounded a bit like a challenge but, before George could query it, the keeper had turned away to direct his beaters.

THE SECOND DRIVE

George was in the centre of the beating line. He kept Nugget to heel rather than letting him work out front. Had he not been shooting, and therefore able to devote more attention to his dog, he would have let him do so, having first ascertained it had the go-ahead from the keeper. Perhaps, if another chance to walk occurred later in the day, he would let Nugget work out in front; by that stage he should have worked off his exuberance and be steady and reliable. He was worried lest the dog go too far out and out of immediate control. He had seen several dogs ruined in this way; not every dog can adjust, on alternate drives, from straight retriever to working dog, quartering the ground, and back to retriever again. Working in front is great fun for a dog and hard work, but there are many potential diversions which may cause the dog to disgrace itself (and its master) by ignoring its master's instructions in its excitement.

George thoroughly enjoyed walking, especially since, on a cold day, it offered the chance to warm up. Also, because he knew nobody would be behind him, he could shoot with reasonable confidence that he was unlikely to shoot someone he did not know was there. That said, he still disciplined himself not to shoot low at birds behind, ensuring that he would only shoot at a bird that was silhouetted against a clear sky. As the beaters began their advance through the covert, George hung back slightly.

Simultaneously, a hare ran in front and then behind him, whereupon he took aim and was about to pull the trigger when he remembered his host's exhortation to spare hares. Almost immediately a rabbit darted out from under a tree stump and, again, George remembered his host's clear direction that no ground game should be shot (14). As the drive continued, George spoke to the beaters either side of him which they appreciated since, as often as not, Guns never spoke to them from one drive to the next. Whether it was coincidence or not, they subsequently seemed to flush a lot of birds which flew in his direction. Fortunately the beaters and Nugget picked his kills because, after a while, he could not mark their whereabouts accurately.

Note: (14) *For safety reasons, ground game really should not be shot on driven shoots. There is far too great a risk of shooting a beater, picker-up or a dog or fellow Gun.*

He was walking along, contemplating the satisfaction of taking part in such a good day, when one of the beaters yelled, 'Cock back!' (15). Instinctively he looked up, saw a woodcock jinking through the trees, raised his gun and, as he was about to fire, saw a second woodcock. He fired at the first, saw it drop and then swung onto the second. It too dropped dead in a bush behind him. Nugget marked the birds and, unlike many dogs who display a manifest distaste for retrieving woodcock, was perfectly happy to do so.

'Good shooting. A right and a left at woodcock is worthy of a knighthood,' said a beater who turned out to be a local doctor, who often came along for the exercise and enjoyment of seeing others doing something well, even though he was not a shooting man. 'I'll be your witness if you like and I'm sure Len there will be your second witness so that you can claim your bottle of whisky from the *Shooting Times*'. George had heard that the *Shooting Times* offered such a prize, as long there were at least two witnesses to the event, but had never met anyone who had won it.

Note: (15) *Woodcock are frequently identified by beaters with the cry 'Cock!' On cock-pheasant-only days, beaters may help the guns by calling 'Hen' or 'Cock.' The author wishes fervently that participants in a shoot, particularly Guns and beaters, be forbidden from shouting 'Woodcock' or 'Cock' since it is an inducement to dangerous shooting because the urgency of the cry seems to make Guns think the woodcock must be shot and are drawn into potentially very dangerous, low shots. Allied to that, woodcock deserve greater respect and should be left alone unless a Gun has the prospect of a safe shot and enjoys eating such a delicacy.*

He did not shoot anything else that drive and would have been content to have finished the day then, even though he realized that there were probably at least two more drives before lunch. He had had great sport already, Nugget had performed immaculately, and it seemed to be tempting fate to go on.

THE THIRD DRIVE

'Dead-eye; eh, George?' said Charles as they met by the trailer again. 'The beaters are positively buzzing about your skill. They say you're incapable of missing. That's good, because you're in a good spot this next drive.'

George suddenly wondered whether such faith and implied responsibility might be over-generosity on Charles' part; somehow, he had an intuition that he might not manage to live up to this heady reputation for much longer. He was a reasonable shot but inconsistent, like the majority of people are, and experienced enough to acknowledge his weaknesses and to recognize the warning signals when he might lose form. Just now, the signals were beginning to flash at him with depressing familiarity.

When the trailer halted, the Guns began to dismount. One of the Guns, instead of handing his gun sleeve containing his gun to someone while he climbed down, kept it in his hand. As he jumped down, he hit the barrels with a dull but audible thud against the tailgate. Without bothering to check his gun he strode off to his peg.

George went to his peg, speculating about the potential severity of the damage to the gun and surprised at the owner's seeming indifference. He was just loading his gun when a pheasant got up in front of the Gun on his left. The bird could not have been more than ten feet from the end of the barrels. There was a great cloud of feathers as if a duvet had been assassinated, and the bird seemed to explode, mutilated beyond recognition. 'What a dreadful waste, not to mention a thoroughly unsporting shot,' mused George to himself, hardly bothering to listen to the perpetrator's blustering excuse: 'Good Lord, did you see that? My shot must have balled.'

George had heard of shot balling, a phenomenon where the shot fuses to form an almost solid ball. This is liable to destroy a bird if it makes contact, but not pluck it, as happens when the bird takes the full force of the standard contents of a cartridge. It is a very rare occurrence indeed. Also, George knew when a bird had been shot at absurdly close range.

Four cocks flew over between him and George, as the man was reloading. George fired at one, which he knew he had hit. Almost simultaneously, there was a shot from his left followed by: 'My bird I think, old man.' George's first reaction was to argue the toss since he was absolutely certain that it was his bird but held his tongue after a moment's hesitation, thinking that a true sportsman would not be so greedily eager to claim the spoils.

It was pointless to argue over something so trivial, even if it happened more than once. More importantly it would have been rude to his host to disrupt the harmony of the day; after all, he knew that the bird had fallen to his gun and that was all that mattered. The Gun on his right, afterwards, whispered knowingly in his ear: 'I reckon that was your bird without a shadow of a doubt. I liked the way you didn't fuss over it.'

George's next bird fell dead almost at Nugget's feet. As he was reloading, there was a streak of black which disappeared even quicker than it had appeared. A black labrador from down the line had stolen the bird from right under Nugget's nose before he could make any protest whatsoever. When the thief reached its master he received a congratulatory pat on the head, instead of the remonstration he should have received. George was not surprised, later, that the owner made no effort to apologize for the dog's appalling behaviour. To compound his crime, the black Lab had eaten the bird at the peg, failing to mark any of his master's own birds as a result (16).

George was more concerned about the standard of his own marksmanship which, as he had suspected, was far from satisfactory all of a sudden. He missed pheasant after pheasant to the extent that Nugget, instead of sitting up alert, lay down and tried to sleep. Up until this moment, George had ignored all the pigeon he had seen – partly because he felt that to shoot a pigeon early in a drive might disturb the pheasants but mainly because experience from rough shooting had ingrained in him the belief that a shot at pigeon almost inevitably scared off the game.

Pigeon are pests but offer extremely tricky, sporting shooting. It takes quite a few to make a decent meal. Thus, before shooting at them, particularly on a formal shoot, it is sensible to decide whether it is worth it. The best thing to do is to ascertain from one's host whether to take pigeon or not. If you do shoot at

---

Note: (16) *It is considered rude to allow one's dog to pick mid-drive, not least because it can be very distracting, both to other Guns and the owner. There will be certain circumstances, although never on the grouse moor, when it is permissible to let a dog pick mid-drive and the direction to do so will be provided by the host. However, pricked birds should be picked up as soon as possible, provided that it is safe to do so.*

a pigeon, you can virtually guarantee that some pheasants will fly over you in perfect formation before you have time to reload.

Anyway, more out of frustration born from desperation, George took a casual shot at a couple of very high pigeons. Hitting one, he fired at the other and was amazed when they both fell to earth quite dead. Nugget sat up, looked at the birds and then at George with a look that seemed to say: 'Wow! What's happened to you, Master?'

Master and dog were disturbed from further telepathic views on pigeon by a great flush of pheasants which broke cover simultaneously, well out of range and closely followed by a large retriever. The dog had broken loose, charged through the covert and driven the bulk of the birds in the covert towards the Guns in one mass. As usually happens in such instances, the birds were not even flushed anywhere near the Guns. It was an object lesson in why dogs should be kept under control, how to ruin a drive, and how to incur the host's displeasure. Such actions are unlikely to result in further invitations.

The drive was virtually over, with the beaters still in cover but obviously very close, when a hen broke cover and flew towards the Gun on George's right. The bird seemed to fly straight at the Gun at about head height. The Gun shot at the bird, missing spectacularly but sending his shot straight into the bushes to his front.

Immediately, there was a cry from behind the bush, more indignant than anything else, 'Hey! That hit me!' As it transpired, fortunately, the beater had been peppered but no shots had penetrated his clothing or skin. The Gun whose fault it was, was profoundly apologetic. He was well-versed in shooting etiquette and, to save Charles the embarrassment of sending him home, went up to his host.

'Charles, I am most terribly sorry. Thank God the beater seems to be unscathed... I am insured though, if need be, but I don't think it'll be necessary. I will take my leave and go home. Thank you for your kind invitation and for such splendid sport. I just pray that I have not completely ruined the day for you.' With that he departed, despite Charles' protestations that no damage had been done and that he should stay (17).

This incident had a salutary effect on everybody else because the Gun was a very experienced shot. 'Just goes to show,' said another Gun finally, 'that it's those of us who think we're ultra-safe, by virtue of age and experience, who are possibly the most dangerous. It certainly proves we're all human...'

Note: (17) *This is a very tricky situation to which there is no easy answer. It is unlikely that the culprit will repeat the error but, whether a guest or member of a syndicate, he should offer to leave, thereby giving his host or captain the choice. The host must be clear and, if the Gun is a guest, either agree to his leaving or insist that he stays. If the shoot is syndicated and the culprit is a member of the syndicate, the captain must make it clear whether the culprit should stay away for evermore or may return the next time. Certainly there would be no question of continuing with that syndicate if he made the same mistake twice. The culprit must make due apologies to his host and victim. If the victim requires medical treatment, the culprit should avoid admitting liability and should seek legal advice as soon as possible.*

THE FOURTH DRIVE (18)

Silence descended while the Guns were driven a couple of miles in the trailer to the grouse butts up on the moor, which formed a large proportion of the estate. The silence was no bad thing, since grouse are very easy to disturb unless great caution is exercised. George made his way through the heather to his butt along a well-trodden path, which was nearly on a flank, with one Gun only on his right. He took stock of his situation.

The butt was built from peat turves on top of stone and provided reasonable shelter from the wind and a degree of concealment from approaching grouse. George settled Nugget in the butt so that he was completely concealed from view to the

---

Note: (18) *This section describes only a driven grouse shoot. Another, more informal method of grouse shooting involves walking-up grouse. Here, Guns walk steadily, taking care for safety's sake to walk straight, line abreast, across a moor, flushing grouse as they go. Guns should not talk except to relay instructions. It can be hard work and calls for alertness and fitness; not a little skill is required in deciding what to carry to avoid carrying too much clobber (clothing, ammunition, gamebag and other impedimenta). Birds can usually be taken to front and behind. Dogs should be kept in to avoid flushing birds out of range, and be used to retrieve downed birds.*
A similar method is to shoot over pointers. Here again, Guns walk up but with pointers quartering the ground well out to the front. The pointers are supposed to stop and point as soon as they scent a bird and should remain absolutely motionless until the Guns are in range, whereupon they (or the noise of the Guns moving through the heather) will flush the quarry.

front. Then he worked out his arcs and marked them with a couple of empty cartridge cases he found in the bottom of the butt. As a precaution, he put his unloaded gun to his shoulder and swung several times between his markers, carefully noting the lie of the land at each extremity of the arc. The idea of this was to give him a firm indication when to swing no further to left or right and, therefore, when to raise his gun and to shoot behind. To swing through and beyond the arcs is called 'swinging through the line' and is extremely dangerous since it means that, at some point, a neighbouring Gun will have a loaded gun pointing at him. George was relieved to notice that his neighbours were doing likewise (19).

Having placed several cartridges to hand on the top of the butt to speed up reloading, he placed his gun conveniently on the top of the butt, so that all he had to do was raise it to his shoulder when the time came. Donning his safety glasses, he stood still but, at the same time, continually swept his arcs with his eyes. He was prepared for a long wait.

The Gun to his left was crouched down below the top of his butt, so that only his eyes and above showed over the top of the butt. To further reduce his silhouette, the Gun kept his barrels below the top of the butt as well. George used to do the same until a canny old keeper told him that grouse are far more likely to be

---

Note: (19) *These days it is highly likely that there will be canes placed either side of butts to discourage Guns from swinging through the line. They are not arc markers, even though, coincidentally, they can be used as such. On some moors, Guns will be issued with canes at the start of the day, frequently elaborate in design, to carry all day and set up in each butt they occupy during the day.*

deterred by the sudden appearance of a Gun popping up from his butt than by somebody in good view but not moving. Nevertheless, George was still careful to maintain a discreet silhouette so that he was not unnecessarily conspicuous. Several coveys flew over Guns up and down the line. George steeled himself not to watch what might be happening, though, experience having taught him that as soon as he was distracted, a covey would fly straight over him while he was looking elsewhere.

George was relieved to discover that his desultory performance in the last drive was only short-lived. That said, he was well aware that grouse-shooting requires completely different techniques to pheasant-shooting. Grouse necessitate the Gun to shoot low, usually with the gun nearly parallel to the ground, something which would result in instant expulsion on a driven pheasant shoot.

He shot five-and-a-half brace of grouse. Several of the birds were shot behind the butt since, once the beaters had appeared, even though technically still well out of range, the head beater had blown a horn indicating that Guns were only to take birds behind until the end of the drive. George, like most experienced grouse shots, imposed his own shoot-behind restriction almost invariably before the horn was sounded in order to avoid the slightest risk of wounding a beater. Unlike the Guns, the beaters stood out well due to the safety flashes they wore. Long before they came into sight, their flags, which they waved to make the grouse fly away from them, gave them away by the distinct, sharp, flapping noise they made.

At the end of the drive Nugget picked all the birds and it was time to drive down to the lodge for lunch. Unexpectedly, Charles announced suddenly: 'Let's not do lunch yet. I would just like to throw in a quick partridge drive.' Conveniently, the partridge drive was just a bit further down the hill from the moor and en route to the lunch venue. After grouse, partridge were George's favourite quarry because they offer such sporting shooting. These days, there are very few grey (or English) partridge shoots since they are truly wild birds and numbers have suffered catastrophically as a result of modern farming methods. Instead, shoots with partridge will rear redlegs or Frenchmen as they are known and thus it was on Charles Shute-Strait's shoot.

The Guns had literally just reached their pegs when the first partridge coveys appeared, some only about 20 feet off the ground but others rising dramatically as they saw the Guns. Partridge seem to fly very fast but, in fact, are usually no faster than pheasant. George, being centre of the gun line had a very fruitful drive, shooting 11 redlegs and one grey which had mingled with a large covey of redlegs; although slightly embarrassed at shooting a grey, George knew that it takes extraordinary powers of observation to differentiate between the partridge species under such circumstances. In passing, it has to be said that greys make for far superior eating to redlegs.

Lunch

Charles Chute-Strait tended to view lunch as a bit of a nuisance: he enjoyed his food, but he enjoyed shooting more. Nevertheless, he recognised the need to give the beaters a rest. Another reason he did not like shooting lunches was because he was concerned that a Gun might drink too much and become distinctly more casual and dangerous as a result. He was even less keen on shooting through and having a late lunch afterwards since it made for a very long day, especially if there was a long drive home afterwards.

This might sound cynical and over-generalised but, over the years, his experience had inexorably led him to this conclusion. Statistics proved that the majority of accidents in the shooting field happened after lunch.

George was of a similar opinion and opted for simple lunches. Usually, he had a pie or pasty, hopefully still warm in its thermal container, and some hot soup for cold days followed by fruit and chocolate. On hot days, he preferred buns and scotch eggs. He also took plenty of bottled water, which he would drink between drives; indeed, on hot days on the grouse moor, it is essential to drink plenty of liquid if one is not to risk becoming dangerously lethargic. George had often drunk two litres in a day, occasionally more. He also took a few biscuits and some water for the dog.

To drink, he took some ginger beer, water, a can or two of beer and sometimes some claret. He rarely touched alcohol when shooting but enjoyed distributing hospitality and found it was a good way to effect a rapport with Guns he might not have got to know in the morning. Nine times out of ten, he found that he took home most of the alcoholic drink he had brought since people are wary of drinking, driving and handling a gun.

THE FIFTH DRIVE

With lunch over quite quickly, Charles was about to direct the guns to the trailer but waited when he noticed two of the Guns in their respective cars, talking on their mobile telephones. Inherent good manners prevented him from displaying the impatience and irritation he felt at this unwarranted delay (20). Meanwhile the other Guns stood and chatted idly (21).

Note: (20) *While it is sad that business cannot always be separated from pleasure, it must never be allowed to interfere in such a situation; if it does, further invitations to shoot will not be forthcoming. If essential, business should be conducted during lunch. It is not unknown for people to carry their telephones with them into the shooting field; it is one of the hallmarks of the age, although, even in the 1920s a few shoot owners apparently installed telephones in their butts! Telephone users should: switch off their telephones and never use them in the middle of drives and wait to use them quietly between drives, but not delay the start of the next drive; ensure that they cannot be telephoned half-way through a drive; and follow the simple principle that the telephone should never be intrusive or disturb the other Guns.*

(21) *Until one reaches one's peg, the gun remains in its slip. Only at the peg is the gun removed, opened as it leaves its slip, and held open over the crook of the arm. If there is a delay at this point, Guns may chat with their neighbouring Gun. When the start of the drive is signalled, usually by a whistle or horn, the Guns return quickly to their pegs, load and close the gun ready for action.*

Eventually, after several minutes, both missing Guns emerged from their cars and rejoined their fellows, neither offering more than a token apology, both seemingly unaware they had done anything untoward. The Guns climbed on to the trailer to be taken to the Bog as it was known. This, as the name implied, was a marshy piece of low-lying moor, adjoining the grouse moor. It held an abundance of snipe and, frequently, a few duck.

The Bog was surrounded by an old sheep fence, topped with barbed wire. This was an awkward obstacle. George turned to a man beside him and asked him if he would be good enough to hold his gun. Before passing the gun, he opened it to show it was unloaded and left it open. Having passed his open gun, he detached his leather protector from his stick and attached it on the top strand of wire. He crossed over the fence and then urged Nugget to leap the fence, over the protector. Another Gun removed his jacket and laid it along the top strand of the fence so that his dog could jump over safely. Some years previously, George had lost a dog that had ripped its belly open on wire which was why he tended to be so pedantic about fences (22). Once all the Guns and beaters were over the fence, they lined up in one long line and advanced

---

Note: (22) *I have had made up a piece of leather 10cm x 60cm (4" x 24"), folded in half with 3 press studs incorporated at either end and one in the middle. This is attached to my stick by a hook and eye and can be removed easily and placed over barbed wire to provide protection for dogs and humans when crossing; equally easily it can be attached to the strap of a gunsleeve. It requires a certain amount of practice to ensure that one's dog actually leaps over the protected piece of fence rather than taking a more hazardous line either side of the protector.*

through the bog. It was tricky going and required one eye firmly fixed on the going and the other peeled for quarry. Everybody stepped from tussock to tussock with much circumspection.

One gun mistook a tussock for terra firma and found himself stepping into icy liquid up to his chest, further downward movement being arrested by his gun wedging across the top of the gap. Laboriously he extracted himself, drained his boots and carefully checked his gun for damage and blocked barrels before continuing.

Two snipe rose in front of George, about five yards apart. Both jinked in that elusive manner unique to snipe before soaring high and out of range. George fired both barrels but missed. Snipe are arguably the most difficult birds to shoot, demanding lightning reactions from the Guns. To compound the problem, they are often hard to find once shot, especially because many dogs refuse to pick them.

Some mallard were rash enough, just then, to fly over. George aimed at one and fired. As it was falling, he fired at another and hit it conclusively, too. Nugget retrieved both subsequently, to his satisfaction.

This drive did not last long but netted several snipe and mallard, George managing to account for two snipe, and three mallard.

THE SIXTH DRIVE

The sixth drive was marred by a fairly dramatic incident. On the way to the drive, after removing his gun from its sleeve, one of the Guns had knocked his barrels hard against a wall. Carelessly, he omitted to check for any damage. Had he done so he would have seen a serious dent in the left barrel.

He fired at several birds without incident because, each time, he only used one barrel. Then he shot at a rabbit which he had no right to shoot anyway after Charles' orders. He missed with the first barrel and then fired immediately with the second.

The rabbit was hit but, simultaneously, the left barrel split, miraculously causing no injury to the firer. Little more was said by anybody since the proof of failing to keep an eye on safety matters was all too plain to see. That Gun, no longer able to use his gun, stayed at his peg until the end of the drive and then, for the seventh and last drive, stood beside Charles.

George was in a good stand. The Guns were lined up in a valley, facing a wood high up on the side of the valley, which produced some very high and testing birds, flying over the Guns before gliding into the cover behind the line on the other side of the valley.

THE SEVENTH DRIVE

The seventh and last drive saw George as a walking Gun again. This time he let Nugget work off the lead, having first sought the keeper's permission.

As they walked up, George kept giving Nugget verbal encouragement with the aims of maintaining remote control over the dog, letting his neighbouring beaters know his whereabouts, and to put up any game along his route.

Having been relatively restrained most of the day, Nugget was greatly relieved to be doing something interesting and actually vastly more exciting than sitting model-dog fashion at the peg. Before long he was working twenty yards out, and then thirty, and then further still. Knowing the implications of letting a dog get too far out, George called his dog to heel only to have him ignore him completely.

Not surprisingly, George was upset. As soon as Nugget came within arm's reach he called him to heel, grabbed him by the ruff (he always took off his collar lest he get caught and, at worst, strangled in the undergrowth because of it) and carefully put down his gun. He then put both hands around Nugget's neck, and shook him firmly but not violently, at the same time looking him in the eye and admonishing his disobedience.

This had the desired effect and a contrite Nugget was once again scrupulous in heeding his master. George, meanwhile, picked up his gun, checking the barrels for any obstructions since they had rested on soft earth, and continued walking. He had plenty of shooting, avoiding taking birds going forwards.

All too soon the drive was over and the Guns were driven back to the house on the trailer. Although, technically, this had been the last drive, George and two other Guns were to stay behind to flight duck as bidden by Charles, once the other Guns had departed.

THE BAG

When the trailer arrived at the house, Jem Morgan was just finishing laying out the bag. George asked him for the details and noted them for his gamebook. He need not have done so because Charles issued cards with the details already inscribed to each Gun. George quietly asked a Gun, whom he knew shot there regularly, what was considered a proper tip (23).

The final tally was 257 Pheasant (171 cocks and 86 hens), 19 brace of Grouse, 29 brace of Partridge (27 Redlegs and 2 of Greys), 7 Woodcock, 14 Snipe, 9 Mallard and 11 Pigeon.

As is customary at the end of the day, Jem Morgan went up to each Gun in turn, rather than the other way round, and handed a brace of pheasants to each and woodcock to those who had shot them – George remembered wondering, as a child, why the bag was not divided equally among the Guns since they had shot

---

Note: (23) *Unless you have been told quite specifically not to by your host or shoot captain, you will be expected to tip the keeper. Beaters will be paid separately. If you have bought the day through an agent you should ask him what is an appropriate tip, otherwise ask a regular member of the shoot. Only ask your host if none of the other Guns know the answer. As to amount, there is no hard and fast rule. Nevertheless, tips on the grouse moor tend to be significantly larger than those on a pheasant shoot.*

them after all (24). The snipe were kept back for Charles. George discreetly shook hands with the keeper, as did the others, palming several notes across into his hand as he did so. He also asked if he could buy a few brace of partridge which Jem was happy to provide for a really very small sum. George was horrified to see one Gun refusing a brace with the words: 'Oh, I don't want any birds, I can't stand eating them'.

As always at this moment at the end of a shoot, he recalled his father's words: 'When you tip the keeper, don't tip him with anything other than a note; coins are for cabbies. And don't wave the tip around, ostentatiously. Be discreet and pass it across in the palm of your hand as you shake hands. And if you've had a good day, don't stint yourself... show your appreciation with a decent tip. Lord knows, a keeper's wage is a pittance and besides, if you see him right, he'll see you right the next time you're invited to shoot if you're that lucky. In fact, he might even help get you invited again... Oh, and by the way, don't be bashful about going to thank the beaters personally. You've no idea how much such a simple gesture is appreciated and that one's free to boot!'

Note: (24) *Once each Gun has been given a brace and other favours fulfilled, the rest of the bag will be sold to a butcher or a game dealer, the income going towards running the shoot. If you would like more birds, as long as you are prepared to offer to pay, do not be shy to ask. Too many people shoot game but are not prepared to eat it, often avoiding taking any home. An innovation on some shoots is to give Guns a dressed (ie plucked and drawn) brace of birds, which will have been shot on a previous shoot and hung for a few days.*

Once they had been given their brace each, the Guns thanked Charles and departed, leaving Charles, George, two other Guns and the keeper. The keeper was rehanging the bag on the racks in the game-cart hitched to the back of his Land Rover, to take it to his game larder, which was a cool room attached at the back of his cottage. The next day, they would be collected by the local game dealer. Ideally, they would be collected early that evening but the impending duck-flight precluded that.

THE DUCK FLIGHT

The light was beginning to fade as Charles led the Guns down to the flighting pond, which was about 500 yards from the house. Everybody was under strict instructions to keep their dogs on the lead, silence being essential (25). When they were close enough to the pond – actually it was more of a small lake – to see the lie of the land but not to be seen, Charles quietly and quickly outlined his plan and a few points of safety.

'Don't shoot anything until you're in position and then only if it is definitely coming in, and in range. Do be careful not to shoot each other. I know it is obvious, but in the gloom it's natural to shoot much lower than one realises. This could result in another Gun being hit directly by shot or, as often happens I gather, by a ricochet off the water. To be shooting that low really is dangerous anyway. Don't leave your hide until you hear my signal of two

---

Note: (25) *Duck are arguably the most sensitive of all birds to danger and, consequently, even greater care has to be taken when moving into position. If any duck are disturbed on the way in and not shot at, there is still a good chance they will return a little later.*

whistle blasts, indicating no more shooting. Also, don't release your dogs until the end of the flight or we'll never know whose birds have been picked and whose haven't.'

'I apologize if I'm teaching you to suck eggs but I'm sure you understand my concern. The other thing is, don't shoot at coots or moorhens as they always seem to fly too low anyway. Nuisance as they are, it'll put off any duck if they hear shooting before they're in range. Right, that's all I've got to say … any questions? If not, I'll now place each of you in turn.'

Charles took each Gun to his hide beside the pond, taking pains to point out where the other Guns would be and the most likely flight path of the duck. The hides were made from 3 pallets nailed together with a primitive bench made from a plank across 2 poles sunk into the ground forming the fourth and open side (26).

George settled Nugget so that he was not in the way, in as dry a spot as he could find; nevertheless the ground Nugget sat on was still damp. George was always diligent in drying off Nugget if

---

Note: (26) *If there are, say, two or three Guns only, it makes sense to pick as the birds are shot. This reduces time spent picking in the dark and improves the chances of finding wounded birds immediately. Odd as it may seem, duck will still come in if a dog is in the water. Intriguingly, also, when there are fewer Guns, it might be more advantageous to eschew a hide and stand in the open; as long as one is quiet and still, ducks will still come in. Under certain circumstances and with two Guns only, on a small pond, it might make sense for the Guns to stand together, again quietly and unmoving, almost shoulder to shoulder, with the left Gun firing at birds on the left, the right Gun firing at birds on the right.*

he ever got wet. Rather than rubbing him with a towel, a process that can temporarily remove much of the coat's natural oils, he used an insulated towelling rug, rather like a horse's New Zealand rug, with a hole for the dog's head and held in place by a velcroed towelling surcingle – this was so much easier and more efficient than the zipped towelling bag he used to use and which caused him to be as wet as his dog by the time he had wrestled Nugget into it.

Having organized Nugget, George then oriented himself, checked his arcs of fire and prepared to wait for the duck, wishing he had a shooting stick which would have been perfect for such a situation. As the light faded, he became restless even though he had only been waiting for half an hour. In the dark there is often a false doubt that perhaps everybody has gone home and left one behind. When should one shoot? Is it best to leave the singleton which often appears first as if reconnoitring for the main flight? (27) All these thoughts and more can play tricks on the mind, leaving the Gun confused and apt to do something careless and rushed when something suddenly appears out of the darkness. This was

---

Note: (27) *One school of thought - the author's mainly - holds that incoming duck send a scout or pair of them, to reconnoitre a pond before coming in to feed and settle for the night. If all seems well, or the scouts are shot and not able to return with any news, the rest will come in, seemingly on the basis that no news is good news. If the scouts are shot at but are missed, and return with bad news, the flight will go elsewhere. This credits duck with sophisticated intelligence, which is doubtful. Nevertheless, whether true or not, it is a point to ponder while awaiting an evening flight.*

why George continually maintained a constant 360-degree vigil, which tended to give him a stiff neck but at least kept him alert.

His patience was eventually rewarded when he heard the faint but unmistakeable noise of mallards' wings moving through the air, a sort of cross between a hum and a whoosh. He craned to catch a glimpse of them, counting twelve dark shapes circling before straightening up and preparing to land. They were faint, black silhouettes against a slightly less black sky. He fired twice and was rewarded with the noise of two smacks as two birds hit the water to his front.

He had just reloaded when he saw the quicker, silent, dark, small shape of a teal dropping onto the water, seemingly from nowhere. He fired, and killed the teal. He was aware that the other Guns had fired. Duck, in ones and twos, continued to flight in every few minutes. George reckoned that most duck flights last about 25 to 30 minutes except when there is a full moon and clear sky, in which case the duck may flight for hours. After 30 minutes there were no more shots but Charles waited another five minutes before blowing his whistle; five minutes that taxed Nugget's patience to the absolute limit. Once the whistle had gone, George sent Nugget into the water.

By the time the Guns had finished, the bag was nine mallard and five teal. George adored teal, especially roasted at breakfast after being stuffed the previous night with port-soaked bread.

The Guns made their way back to the house. Before departing, they had a drink with their host who generously gave each a teal and a couple of mallard. George installed Nugget in his towelling rug before letting him leap into the back of the car.

LATER

As soon as he arrived home, George checked Nugget for thorns, scratches and ailments before feeding him. After hanging his birds in an outhouse, he mixed a generous whisky and soda, before setting to cleaning his gun. Once the gun was clean, he cleaned and put away his other equipment before having a good soak in the bath.

When he came down from his bath he wrote up his gamebook and then wrote a thank-you letter to Charles Chute-Strait. In particular, he praised the organization and the variety, and emphasized both his and Nugget's appreciation for his host's generosity. He preferred to write immediately because the day was still fresh in his mind and, more importantly, it showed that he appreciated his host's thoughtfulness and consideration; nothing was ruder, to his mind, than the late letter sent many days or even weeks later, which implied a cavalier casualness and lack of real appreciation of a kindness bestowed.

He went to bed feeling well-satisfied with a wonderful day, and, just as he was about to go to sleep, he realized with pleasure that he had managed to equal the Feudal Park record of the number of game species shot in a day.

2. THE BEGINNER

A Father's Advice

If a sportsman true you'd be,
Listen carefully to me.

Never, never let your gun
Pointed be at anyone;
That it may unloaded be
Matters not the least to me.

When a hedge or fence you cross,
Though of time it cause a loss,
From your gun the cartridge take
For the greater safety's sake.

If 'twixt you and neighbouring gun
Bird may fly or beast may run,
Let this maxim e'er be thine:
'Follow not across the line.'

Stops and beaters, oft unseen,
Lurk behind some leafy screen;
Calm and steady always be;
'Never shoot where you can't see'.

Keep your place and silent be;
Game can hear, and game can see;
Don't be greedy. Better spared
Is a pheasant, than one shared.

You may kill, or you may miss,
But at all times think of this –
'All the pheasants ever bred
Won't repay for one man dead.'

Mark Beaufoy

This chapter is not just for the beginner, young and old, but also for the beginner's tutor, for use as a memory jogger. It does not pretend to be completely exhaustive but should provide a fairly thorough basis for tuition. A good start for all beginners, and indeed the more experienced, if they do not know it, is to memorize the poem *(previous page)*. Written in 1909 by Mark Beaufoy MP for his 13-year-old son Henry, it encapsulates all the essential safety points of shooting.

SAFETY

The chapter on safety in this book says enough, hopefully. Safety, though, is the foundation of all shooting tuition. As the late Major John Ruffer, author and renowned shooting coach used to maintain, a person can be taught to shoot perfectly in ten shots – it is just that most people fail to do what they have been taught thereafter. Thus, the mechanics of shooting are actually but one small facet of learning to shoot.

THE QUARRY

Too often people shoot without a thought for their quarry. It is only a fortunate few who can benefit from accompanying a professional keeper throughout the season to learn about game, rearing game, respect for game, and shooting lore in general. Even then, fewer still learn to respect the environment in which the game lives, unlike the case in Germany, for example.

In Germany, the shooting environment, almost invariably forest, is tended and treated with some reverence – the *forstmeister* or head forester, of a district is held in similar (or greater) esteem than, say, a GP in Great Britain. The Germans believe that if one looks after the environment, Nature will take its course and game will flourish accordingly and be better for it. There is much merit in this philosophy, relying as it does on wild rather than reared game.

In Great Britain, we have destroyed much of our forests and have had to plant special coverts just to hold birds. We have not planted the coverts for the improvement of the environment necessarily, but rather in order to be able to provide cover for an artificially-reared quarry. That said, these days, the majority of estates and shoots are very conservation oriented with shooting taking second priority to conservation. With political pressure on the shooting of reared birds, there is a gradual swing to shoots which encourage wild birds, which must be the way ahead if gameshooting is to be allowed to continue.

Thus it is essential that the beginner should learn as much about game species, pest species and protected species as possible, before shooting any game. At the risk of being repetitive, a German is not allowed to shoot without a permit, which can only be obtained after expensive, long and detailed formal teaching in all aspects of game shooting. While they might not shoot any more accurately than the average (indeed, Germans are more oriented towards ground game than feathered game) at least, theoretically, they know a great deal about their sport.

Whether or not we should adopt a similar system is not in the remit of this book. Nevertheless, it may be imposed on us if newcomers to gameshooting are not properly prepared beforehand, either through their own efforts or someone else's tuition; after all, it is necessary to train in order to obtain a licence for driving a motor vehicle, which is no more or less dangerous than a shotgun.

THE YOUNG BEGINNER

With luck the young beginner or child will have the benefit of a father or other experienced adult tutor from whom to learn shooting lore. With a child, there is usually so much more time in which to learn – the author began by taking his three-year-old son through the steps to be taken on arrival home after a day's shooting. In this way, care of gun and dog, and attention to safety, will become second nature.

Some teaching guidelines follow. It is impossible to stipulate at what age a child can start to shoot with a shotgun. Much depends on the child's size and strength. The author's son who is averagely built, used a .410 for two years from the age of eight before progressing to a 20 bore. There is a significant leap from a 20 bore to a 12 bore in weight and recoil and it may be that the child does not make the transition until the mid-teens. While a .410, or 28 bore, which is nearly the same as a .410 but more effective, is actually rather puny but still potentially very dangerous if mishandled, a 20 bore is virtually as effective as a 12 bore. As long as a gun fits its user, there is no rush to progress to a 12 bore.

It is natural for children to want to emulate their parents but, if a child is patently not interested in guns, do not press the point. Fortunately, children who like playing with guns, once taught, tend also to enjoy demonstrating how to handle them safely.

Start as young as possible – the author fired an air rifle at the age of seven. Instructing a pupil is also the best way to repolish one's own skills.

When a child is able to manage a whole day in the shooting field, let him accompany you, unarmed, to see what happens, and if not on your own land, clear it with your host first. All the better in some respects, incidentally, if he occasionally sees things that should not happen, so long as it is explained why such incidents are wrong.

Later on, take the child along as a shadow, carrying an empty gun all day but going through the motions as if the gun is loaded, e.g. taking out the cartridges before crossing an obstacle. The author's grandfather underwent such a grounding for two seasons before being allowed to load his gun. Two seasons may be excessive, but the point is that no person should be allowed into the shooting field with a loaded gun unless he is as safe as can reasonably be expected. More importantly, if accompanied by a child, explain every shot you take so that the child will learn what is a safe shot, what is a sporting shot, what is unacceptable etc. Also, where practicable, give a running commentary on the shooting from other Guns but beware of being derogatory, on the basis that children have an exceptional ability to pass on comments to the commented on, in the most embarrassing manner imaginable – '..out of the mouths of babes and sucklings...' In this way only can a child really gain essential knowledge.

Do not let a child shoot game until he is totally confident with his gun, able to hit clays accurately and consistently, and able to judge consistently and accurately what is a suitable range at which to shoot birds.

Once a child is shooting, do not tolerate any lapses in behaviour, particularly regarding safety. Any lapses in safety must result in going back to carrying an empty gun for a trial period in order to emphasize the value of safety and that shooting is a privilege, not a right. Supervision by an experienced shot is critical; a willing parent with no shooting experience is not a sensible alternative. The supervisor should accompany the child throughout the day and all shooting days until he is totally confident in the child's ability to consistently judge instinctively what is safe or otherwise. It must be stressed that the supervisor should not attempt nor even intend to shoot alongside the child because he must be able to concentrate totally on his charge the whole time; therefore, he should not be armed at all.

THE ADULT BEGINNER

The adult beginner is at a disadvantage since, very often, he does not have the chance to learn shooting lore over a period of years; at worst, he may be trying to learn shooting within a few days or less in order to fulfil an invitation to shoot. He can go to any shooting school and learn how to fire a gun reasonably accurately, but he is unlikely to learn much else except a few essential points of safety. Unfortunately, probably it will not be practicable to undergo the sort of training for a child as described above. The following is the best advice, albeit limited, that can be offered.

Under no circumstances, if you have never shot before should you accept an invitation unless you are sure that you can fit in some formal coaching at a shooting school beforehand. Also you must inform your potential host. If time permits, or if, having taken up gameshooting, you really want to approach the subject properly, you should attend a BASC Training course. These courses are outstandingly good and, while they do not turn out instant experts, they do produce an extremely comprehensive foundation on which to build experience. There is a basic course for novices. *The address of BASC is on page 165*.

Do not be afraid to seek the advice of others and do not be too proud to heed it. Trust others and do not deviate from their advice until you have gained experience and can therefore judge for yourself – at one extreme, their advice should stop you from dressing outrageously but more pertinently from perpetrating a dangerous act.

Go to a shooting school and practise until you are consistently accurate.

Equip yourself only with essentials, bearing in mind that you may not wish to continue shooting after your initial experience. You may need to borrow a gun, but do not borrow one other than from a knowledgeable source or unless it has been checked and certified as being safe – it may not hurt you but could hurt somebody else. For a small fee, you may be able to persuade a gunsmith to hire you a gun, or to check one borrowed from an inexpert source. If you are a certificate holder and you borrow it for more than 72 hours, both the lender and yourself must give the appropriate notices to the local chief of police concerned within seven days. If you do not have a shotgun certificate, you may only borrow a gun from the owner on their private land and in their presence. If you are under 18 years of age, further restrictions apply.

If the opportunity presents itself, accompany a friend as often as possible beforehand to learn what a day's shooting involves. As an old military adage goes, 'Time spent in reconnaissance is seldom wasted'.

Do not accept an invitation unless you can fulfil your obligations as a guest, i.e. only accept if you can definitely make the day; also, do not be too proud to admit to being totally inexperienced since, in all probability, it will be apparent the moment you set a foot out of your car on arrival at the shoot. If you have never shot before on a formal shoot, or even only once or twice, you must as a matter of courtesy inform your host. Instantly you will gain some respect for your humility but if you say nothing, you could easily end up inviting contempt since, inevitably, your inexperience will show through, however much you think you might be able to conceal it. Thereafter, if you have any queries ask your host but, if it is during a drive, seek advice from a neighbour, although not once the birds start to come over.

THE GAMESHOOTER'S TEN COMMANDMENTS

John Marchington, the well-known shooting author and sportsman, composed the 'commandments' below, which could form the foundation of all gameshooters' interest in their sport. Time spent learning these and Mark Beaufoy's poem (p37) will not be wasted.

1. Be at all times <u>safe</u>.
2. Always strive to achieve clean kills by avoiding over-long range shooting.
3. Retrieve and despatch wounded game as soon as possible.
4. Place the well-being of your dog before your own.
5. Study to be quiet.
6. Avoid greediness, taking neither unsporting shots nor indulging in excessive killing.
7. Avoid selfishness – let others have the sport which is rightly theirs.
8. Never shoot at quarry you cannot completely see.
9. Respect and conserve the natural scene.
10. Regard shooting as a means to an end, not an end in itself.

SHOOTING WITH A PAIR OF GUNS

If a person is told to bring a pair of guns when invited to shoot, it means that he can expect a great deal of fast shooting at a very large number of birds. Such days are relatively rare and the beginner is unlikely to be faced with such an opportunity; this short section is included just in case this happens, though.

It will be necessary to take considerably more ammunition than normal. It is impossible to say how much, but take a couple of 250-cartridge packs. Obviously two guns are needed. Dress needs to be smart and formal, in all likelihood. Normally, loaders will be provided by your host, but do check.

Technique

If participating in a two-gun day for the first time, it would be imprudent not to seek the advice of an expert with whom you can also practise changing guns. Any good shooting school should be able to help but, before booking a lesson, establish that the school has the necessary expertise. What follows is for right-handers and, in principle, should be reversed for left-handers.

The loader should stand to your right and slightly behind. He will hold your second, loaded gun in his right hand.

Once you have fired your first gun, you apply the safety-catch; this is most important, especially if only one barrel has been fired – and hand it with your right hand to your loader's left hand.

You take the second gun from your loader's right hand with your left hand.

Do not, either of you, try to cut corners as far as safety is concerned. Thus, make sure your loader knows you will only accept a gun from him with the safety-catch at Safe.

At the end of a drive both of you should unload the gun you are holding, and prove it to each other.

To conclude, it is vital that you establish an immediate rapport with your loader, if he is a stranger to you, and let him know precisely what you expect from him. Practise changing and perfect your technique before the first drive. Finally, if your loader has been provided by your host, do not forget to tip him or her – a sum at least equal to the tip to the keeper.

3

THE HOST

Introduction

The success of a day's shooting depends very much on the skill and good manners of the host, or shoot captain in the case of a syndicate shooting land it has rented. It is not intended to describe in pedantic detail how a host should behave but, rather, to say what a guest should reasonably expect from his host.

There are hosts and hosts, as the following true story illustrates: A friend of the author's, while studying agriculture at Reading University, was once asked to shoot somewhere in Berkshire, by a fellow student. The invitation included all the details he needed such as timings, where to meet, what to bring, etc. On arrival, he found several other Guns and a good-sized party of beaters already there. After an excellent initial briefing by their host, everybody went and took their respective places for the first drive. Each stand was beautifully pegged and it was quite obvious that a great deal of preparation had gone into the day.

The morning's shooting was thoroughly enjoyable and everybody was in fine form by lunchtime. It was during lunch that the author's friend turned to his host and remarked casually, 'I didn't know that you owned land in Berkshire. I thought all yours was in Sussex.'

'You're absolutely right. No, I saw this land the other day and thought it promised some good shooting so planned a day's shooting accordingly. . .', entirely without the owner's consent, as it turned out.

WHAT DOES A GUEST EXPECT FROM HIS HOST?

His invitation should include a time and place to meet, with sufficiently detailed directions to get there (send an extract of a map if necessary), whether any meals will or will not be provided, whether or not dogs are welcome, whether to bring more than one gun and, if so, whether to bring a loader and whether or not to bring a friend or companion, although if not mentioned it is pretty safe to assume that the invitation does not extend beyond oneself.

At the meet, the host should introduce any strangers.

The initial brief should be firm, positive, unambiguous, precise and succinct, so that each Gun knows exactly what the outline plan for the day is, what to shoot and any particular limitations on conduct, including points of safety and the numbering of Guns at stands. Among briefing details, Guns should be asked to pick up their empty cartridge cases after each drive: to this end there should be a bucket or similar receptacle in which empties may be thrown.

Where practicable, the host will mark each stand with a peg or stick with a number on it. This gives a clear indication where a Gun should stand and some pegs are also substantial enough to provide an anchor for tethering a dog. But never underestimate the ability of even a cocker to smash pegs when sufficiently excited. For this reason it is absolutely forbidden to attach a dog to oneself when shooting. Many Guns bring a device which screws into the ground and is virtually immovable. Grouse butts should also be equipped with a dog-anchoring hook or sturdy nail over which a lead can be slipped to prevent the dog being able to escape.

Throughout the day, the host should be running the show unobtrusively, ready to alter plans if necessary – after due consultation with his keeper, a courtesy sometimes forgotten. If he changes his plan, he must remember to inform all who might possibly be affected by the changes.

The unselfish host will devise a system of numbering so that each Gun has equal opportunities of shooting throughout the day. If he intends to shoot, he will also avoid the temptation to put himself in all the best stands, instead taking his turn with his guests. He will studiously ensure that all guests get something to shoot at.

The host will ensure birds are presented in such a way that they provide a demanding test of skill, which is compatible with the ability of the Guns. He should aim for quality of bag and not quantity. It is not in the remit of this book to lay down what is an excessive bag – a few shoots achieve bags of many hundreds of pheasants and present the most testing shooting over the heads of the finest shots in the country. What is an excessive figure is hard to quantify, although there are commercial shoots prepared to sacrifice quality for quantity with scant respect for the quarry. It's worth remembering the old adage that if you can't remember every bird you've shot, you've maybe shot too many.

At the end of the day the host will ensure shooting stops at least an hour before sunset to allow pickers-up to complete their task before birds go to roost. He (and his keeper) will also ensure that guests leave with a brace of good birds each. He will thank (and pay) the beaters and have a detailed debrief with his keeper thereafter.

It is essential that the host is firm and confident, so that he inspires confidence in his guests. It is perhaps worth remembering that guests, and indeed all present, want to know what they have to do and that, therefore, they expect to be told what to do. Also, guests and Guns, alike, expect their host to take positive steps to maintain safety should safety ever be jeopardized.

THE CODE OF GOOD SHOOTING PRACTISE

A Code of Good Shooting Practise has been drawn up jointly by BASC, Countryside Alliance and Game and Wildlife Conservation Trust (GWCT). This code can only be effective if shoot owners and captains, and gameshooters, abide by it and take positive action to help eliminate any malpractices.

Golden Rules

The Code of Good Shooting Practise is a mixture of objective and subjective judgements and standards.

The objective standards are enshrined in the following principle:

> *'Rearing and releasing of game for shooting should only be done in order to provide a sufficient stock of game, fully adapted to the wild, which can be sustained without damage to the environment or to the wild stock.'*

THREE GOLDEN RULES OF SHOOTING

evolve from this principle:

1. No birds shall be released after the start of annual shooting in the area concerned and they shall not be shot until they are fully adult and well-adapted to the wild. Pheasant should be released at least one month before the commencement of shooting; partridge and duck at least 14 days. In practice, the norm for releasing birds is three months.

2. No bird previously released shall be caught up subsequently during its shooting season for re-release during that season.

3. No more birds shall be released in an area of woodland, game cover, or pond than the area can hold without detriment to the health of the birds or to the environment.

4

SAFETY

This book's main aim is to preach safety. No-one denies the influence of fate, but usually it intervenes only after some form of carelessness. Genuine accidents do happen but usually due to negligence by someone and not on the part of the victim.

There are four areas of safety; the points under each heading are not necessarily in a set order of priority. In order to press the point, this chapter is necessarily clipped and curt, hence the simplest classification of Do's and Don'ts.

1. GUNS AND AMMUNITION

Do maintain and service your gun carefully.

Don't use a gun you know to be unsafe.

Don't buy a gun unless you have a reputable gunsmith's certificate to say that it is in proof and safe.

Don't open a gun after a misfire unless it is pointed well away from people and dogs.

Don't mix different calibres of ammunition in pockets or any other container since dangerous barrel bursts can occur.

Don't place ammunition too close to dampness or excessive heat.

Do use the correct size shot for your intended quarry.

Don't use damaged ammunition – remember that a life is worth more than the few pence of a cartridge. Similarly, be very wary of buying or accepting second-hand ammunition. While it may be perfectly safe, it could prove to be unreliable.

Don't use ammunition which the gun has not been proved for, e.g. Magnum cartridges in standard chambers.

Don't ever be complacent.

2. ON THE ROAD

Do keep guns and ancillary equipment which might advertise the presence of guns, hidden and secure, especially when the vehicle is unattended. A surprising number of spare guns left unattended in vehicles during shoots are stolen each year. You can be prosecuted for failing to keep your gun secure and, more critically, the police might withdraw your shotgun certificate.

Don't travel with a loaded weapon.

Do lock your vehicle whenever it is unattended.

Don't be complacent.

3. AT HOME

Do keep photographs of your gun(s) and records of their serial numbers in a safe place, such as another house or, even better, in the bank.

Don't store guns and ammunition together.

Don't leave an assembled gun where children can reach it.

Don't load a gun indoors.

Do lock guns out of sight, ideally in a proper gun cabinet. Although, technically, a gun cabinet is not a legal requirement, many police forces insist that shotguns are kept in a purpose-built gun cabinet.

Do always check a gun is unloaded before handling it.

Do not be complacent.

4. IN THE FIELD

Don't ever allow a gun to be pointed at anyone whether it is unloaded or not.

Don't carry a gun trailing – the barrel may be jabbed into the ground or a trigger could be snagged on an obstruction, with fatal consequences.

Don't carry a gun so that it is pointing at anyone.

Don't carry a loaded gun over your shoulder. Avoid doing this with an unloaded gun too (it should be broken or in a sleeve), since it is easy to swing your gun unwittingly into anybody close behind.

Don't shoot ground game to the front on a driven shoot, that is assuming the host has said that ground game may be shot.

Don't ever shoot low birds or those that are too close.

Don't swing down or through the line.

Don't be greedy; choose targets discriminatively.

Don't change position once placed. Stand still and remain silent. In the rare event that you are told to move, ensure Guns either side know your new position.

Don't pick up birds half-way through a drive. Releasing a dog to retrieve in the middle of a drive potentially can be seriously disruptive to the outcome of the drive and, at the least, a distraction to its owner or the other Guns. If there is a runner or a badly pricked bird, a picker-up will usually deal with it.

Don't ever tie a dog to you – in its excitement as birds appear and you start shooting, it could unbalance you while you have a loaded gun with the safety catch off, which could have catastrophic consequences.

Don't drink too much – most accidents happen after lunch.

Don't fiddle with the safety catch and triggers when your gun is loaded.

Don't hand a gun to someone without first showing them it is unloaded.

Don't shoot unless the whole target is visible i.e. silhouetted against a clear, uninterrupted sky.

Don't shoot into cover.

Don't shoot once the end of a drive has been indicated.

Don't lean a gun against anything (cars, trees, etc.) or leave it on top of a car.

Don't knock your barrels or anybody else's, since they dent very easily and can be expensive to rectify.

Don't shoot if you are losing your balance in any way.

Don't rest the tips of barrels on your feet as they can easily slip off and be damaged if on hard standing or become blocked by mud if on soft ground.

Don't ever load a gun unless you intend to use it, i.e. only load once the drive has started.

Do unload immediately a drive ends.

Do carry your gun over your forearm, open and pointing at the ground. Unless in a sleeve, this is accepted as the best way to carry a gun. Carry it empty unless you are actually walking up game.

Do frequently check the safety catch is on.

Do check the barrels are clear before loading at the start of each drive.

Do look through the barrels if there is the slightest chance that they may have become blocked by mud, snow or anything else.

Do close the stock to the barrels and not barrels to stock. This way the barrels are always pointing at the ground, and the cartridges cannot fall out.

Do check the gun is unloaded at the end of a drive and again before putting in a sleeve, case or car.

Do break your gun (open it) if somebody approaches you while you are standing at your peg.

Do keep a gun broken and empty when in company between drives.

Do remove cartridges before crossing any obstacle such as a stream or fence – merely opening a loaded gun is not sufficient.

Do check a gun is unloaded on receiving it, unless the person handing it over has made this clear already by showing you.

Do point barrels in the air when beaters come into sight towards the end of a drive. This indicates you have seen them and prevents swinging the gun up through them.

Do watch others lest they are dangerous. You may not be able to say much but at least you will be alert to possible dangers.

Do be insured. Membership of BASC gives automatic cover of £10,000,000.

Do listen carefully to your host's or shoot captain's briefings.

Do ensure that you have a valid, up-to-date shotgun certificate. Any changes of address, even within the same police division, must be notified to the police immediately. An invalid shotgun certificate means the owner is breaking the law and, therefore, this will invalidate any relevant insurance policies he or she holds.

Do avoid being complacent; the second you think you're foolproof safe is the moment when you will do something you could regret for evermore.

Many of the points mentioned here have been the cause of an accident at some time, some more than others. Do not add to the list; it is far too long as it is.

Finally, as mentioned already, it is worth reflecting that we do not go shooting to risk our lives...

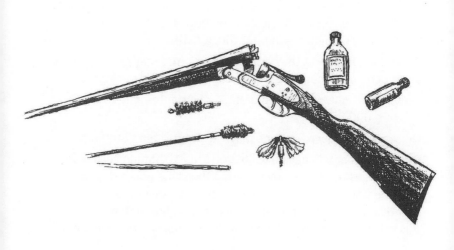

5

CARE OF THE GUN

Care of your gun comes second only to care of your dog. Gun cleaning should be a rigid discipline that happens as soon as you arrive home after a day's shooting – nothing rusts faster than a gun brought inside damp. A few minutes simple effort may save much unnecessary expense and even life.

Failure to clean a gun will result, almost immediately, in the deposits from fired cartridges in the barrels etching into the steel and causing pitting which weakens the barrels. Water causes instant rust on all bare metal parts but is most dangerous in those crevices under the extractors, in and around the action and either side of the rib. Remember that oil can seal in moisture which will result in rust and damage to the gun very quickly. Blood and salt water should be removed the instant they are discovered in the shooting field, since they are about the most corrosive agents likely to be encountered.

What may seem like a tedious and elaborate ritual on first acquaintance, surprisingly enough soon becomes a quick, simple, satisfying and almost automatic habit. If you care for your gun properly, it should serve you for your and probably your children's lifetimes; if you do not, somebody could be maimed or even killed.

CLEANING EQUIPMENT

It is easy to buy a comprehensive cleaning kit very cheaply, which will cover all everyday cleaning needs. Do ensure, though, that you buy the **correct-sized** cleaning kit for the bore of your gun.

The following is a comprehensive list of cleaning equipment:

Comprehensive Gun Cleaning Kit

Beeswax wood polish

Boresnake cleaner

Cleaning rods*

Cleaning rod attachments: Wool mop, Phosphor bronze, Turk's Head steel brush, pullthrough loop*

Cloth patches*

Cotton cleaning rag

Oil: thick and thin varieties or a combined gun cleaner and lubricant*

Polishing duster

Paradox gun cleaner

Small, stiff, bristle (not plastic) brush, e.g. a trimmed ½" paintbrush

Set of turnscrews

Tissues or soft lavatory paper

A clean, dry, safe place for keeping the gun after cleaning

These items comprise the average cleaning kit set.

Routine/End of Day Cleaning

When cleaning any gun, follow these principles:

1. Prove the gun is unloaded before doing anything else.
2. Strip the weapon to a logical sequence. Since most guns consist of three main parts only, this applies to more than routine stripping and cleaning and, unless the weapon has detachable sidelocks, further stripping will be limited to the extractors.

    Leave anything else to a gunsmith.
3. Use the correct tools and cleaning equipment correctly.
4. Place weapon components in a clean, dry, safe place.
5. Do not use undue force in dismantling or assembly. Again, this would normally only apply if the weapon is being stripped beyond its main components.

    If you cannot unscrew a pin (the technical term for a gunscrew) leave it to a gunsmith.

THE SEQUENCE OF CLEANING WILL BE:

The Stock

Wipe away any moisture and dirt from the action and wood with a clean cloth. **On no account ever rub the woodwork with an oily cloth.** Oil rots the woodwork and therefore must be used sparingly on the action so that it does not seep into the woodwork.

If the woodwork is of the oil-finished (linseed type) variety, rubbing a hand over the surface will usually return its appearance to normal again, otherwise apply a little linseed oil.

If the woodwork is French-polished, then treat it with best quality beeswax furniture polish.

Clean the chequering (intended to aid grip) with a soft bristle brush (the ½" paintbrush).

Wipe exposed parts of the action with a very lightly oil-impregnated cloth, once you have removed any dirt and the deposits which tend to gather on the face of the breech, with a phosphor-bronze brush. Even if the gun has become soaked, **on no account should you try to inject oil into the action via the firing pin slots**. It will not counter the action of any moisture but merely find its way into the woodwork like water into a sponge and seal in corrosive moisture. If the gun has been properly serviced and stored correctly, the internal mechanism will be protected from moisture by a film of grease, and moisture will evaporate harmlessly.

The Fore-end

Wipe the woodwork and metal parts with a clean cloth. Use the bristle brush on the chequering if necessary. Wipe the metal parts with a very fine film of oil from a lightly oil-impregnated cloth.

The Barrels

Wipe the outside clean and dry, paying particular attention to the rib, since this is a bad water trap – once rust gains a hold, eventually it will cause the rib to separate from the barrels, rendering the gun unsafe.

Remove any dirt from behind the ejectors with a small piece of rag. Usually it is sufficient to remove the ejectors (by removing the screw (pin) on the underside of the barrels) once in the middle of, then at the end of, the season, or if the gun has been soaked. Using a cotton wool bud or pipe-cleaner, remove any dirt and moisture from the extractor bed. Oil the parts lightly before replacing them.

Unless you have a Paradox cleaner or a Boresnake, an effective method for cleaning the inside of the barrels is as follows. Take three pieces of soft lavatory paper or other tissue and roll into a wad which fits fairly tightly into the chamber. Push the wad through the barrels with your cleaning rods with one smooth, uninterrupted movement. This will remove all but the most stubborn deposits. Then, using the wool mop or pull-through attachment, lightly oil the barrels. Ensure the tissue wad is a good fit but not too tight, or else you could damage the barrels if you have to use excessive force to push the wad through.

For really stubborn deposits, use the turk's head steel brush; for less stubborn deposits use the phosphor bronze brush, ideally with a cleaning patch wrapped round it. Try to use the turk's head sparingly because excessive use could damage the barrels. Incidentally, always check the fittings on cleaning rods for any proud or burred edges. On no account use damaged rods since they will score the barrels irreversibly.

Wipe the outside of the barrels with a thin film of oil, reassemble and put away the gun.

If your gun has been rained on, even though you have cleaned it, check it the next day and in particular operate the safety catch and top lever several times since most of these parts' components are concealed and could rust very easily. Bear in mind that oil can trap any undiscovered dampness, which can result in rust developing, hence the need to consider dry cleaning.

Dry Cleaning

If you are using a gun frequently, **and** your gun cabinet is in a guaranteed dry, damp-free location, it is perfectly acceptable to dry clean your gun i.e. you do not need to apply any oil.

End-of-Season Cleaning and Preservation

Always clean the gun extra carefully at the end of the season; it is not so much the cleaning as the preservation that is important. Strip and clean the gun normally but ensure the metal is well oiled and wood well polished. Store in a secure, cool, dry, airy place (beware of cellars, though) in a gun cabinet. Avoid placing a gun cabinet close to warm radiators, and other sources of heat.

If intending to store a gun assembled, in a gun cabinet, it is logical to place it in the cabinet barrels uppermost. Beware, though: excessive oil, over time, runs downwards and eventually through the firing pin holes into the wood of the stock, where it will cause rot. To obviate this, only oil the barrels lightly and check them from time to time.

Servicing

It is wise to have a gun serviced every two years, unless you have shot very regularly or the gun has been soaking wet, in which cases it should be done every year. Do not economize on this aspect since a gunsmith's inspection may nip a potential (and dangerous) disaster in the bud, which might otherwise only manifest itself at the worst possible moment. An example might be finding rust along the rib, or detecting the effects of rust and wear on firing pins, both eventualities unlikely to be spotted by the owner.

Out-of-Season Cleaning

Check your gun every two months or so and re-oil as necessary. Oil moves, and metalwork could then be exposed to humidity and rust.

Situating a Gun Cabinet

There are two main considerations when installing a gun cabinet. First, if at all possible, it should be concealed from view, ideally within a cupboard. Second and equally important, do not install it where there is the slightest risk of dampness, not least in a cellar; a cellar, however dry you think it may be, should be avoided at all costs because there is no such thing as a damp-free cellar.

6

DRESS AND EQUIPMENT

Your intentions, when dressing and equipping yourself, should be to be comfortable, to blend in seamlessly with your natural surroundings and to conform with your companions. Rather in the way that a person joins a club on its terms, so the guest has a certain obligation to conform to his host's desires within the bounds of common sense and propriety.

This chapter will help the beginner to avoid that minefield which is littered with opportunities for self-embarrassment, but it is not a failsafe for those with an unerringly eccentric eye for the unconventional. It should be pointed out at this stage that while it is not smart to look deliberately and conspicuously scruffy, dressing in completely new kit from top to toe renders the wearer equally conspicuous.

The British tend to draw some comfort from things that are old and well-established, be it their stately homes, their family heirlooms, best English guns or whatever. Such things have an intrinsic value in that they are tried, tested and have proved their reliability and trustworthiness. Anything new is unproven and therefore, until it has proved itself, it will often be treated with varying degrees of suspicion and diffidence. The beginner, therefore, can help himself (and his confidence) by not looking too fresh from the factory without having to look scruffy.

DRESS

Head

A hat serves several purposes. It can prevent the loss of 40% of the wearer's body heat; it will camouflage the balding or snowy tonsure and, finally, it will offer protection from the wind, rain and sun. The standard tweed flat cap is *de rigueur* – simple and without embellishment. There is no need to be tempted by moleskin, waxed cotton or other non-tweed varieties of flat cap. A trilby gives better protection from the rain but is less stable in a wind. Avoid also porkpies, deerstalkers and sou'westers, which are not really suitable. If your jacket comes with a hood, make sure it can be detached and do so. Hoods narrow your vision, impede your hearing and, therefore, are potentially dangerous.

Ears

Some form of ear-defender should always be worn while shooting. Ear-defenders vary from the electronic, amplifying headphone type down to simple foam ear-plugs. Electronic headphones are clever in that they have volume controls for each ear and can amplify sound but also automatically shut out sound, such as the noise of the wearer's gun being fired, thereby preventing damage to the ears. They are not overly expensive and worth the money.

When choosing electronic headphones, avoid those with over-bulbous profiles since they will get in the way of the stock as it comes fully into the shoulder, and buy green or brown ones. Electronic headphones are awkward to carry and their mechanisms are vulnerable to damage if worn in rain. It is possible to buy a waterproof, zipped pouch specially designed for carrying headphones, which can be attached to a cartridge bag or gun sleeve strap and which virtually eliminates the problem of where to carry them without fear of losing them.

Another type, still very expensive but offering the best protection of any form of ear-defender, is a digital plastic plug, moulded to an individual's ears. A cheaper option is a non-digital version but, while extremely effective as protection, these tend to muffle sound which is disconcerting.

Foam ear-plugs are basic but surprisingly efficient and very cheap, costing a few pence. Nevertheless, it is worth spending a few pounds on a pair of silicon rubber ear-plugs with sonic valve inserts. They are extremely effective – indeed, they allow in sufficient sound to be worn while duck-flighting where the gameshooter relies as much on hearing as sight, since flighting generally takes place in poor light – they last ages and can be carried easily in a pocket. The author keeps a pair in each of his various shooting coats because they are effective in any shooting scenario, not least when rain precludes wearing electronic ear-defenders.

Remember that, while ear-defenders' main purpose is to protect hearing by eliminating the damaging decibel frequencies, the wearer must still be able to hear other sounds, not least voices, approaching game or beaters, because it is dangerous to wear something which prevents the wearer from hearing anything at all. As a point of interest, it is a well-established fact that shooting quickly damages unprotected ears beyond repair – just a few shots can inflict permanent damage which will manifest itself in later years. Hearing in the left ear will be affected first in the person who shoots off his right shoulder and vice versa, since this will be the ear most exposed to muzzle blast.

Face

By all means wear a silk or woollen scarf in extremes of weather. Balaclavas and variants are out except for maybe wildfowling and duck-flighting and even then are hardly necessary, particularly since, like hoods, they inhibit the senses. It is possible to try too hard to blend in. Hence military face-veils (which also double as scarves) should be avoided; apart from other considerations, they scratch and snag easily when walking through thick undergrowth. They are however useful for wildfowling and pigeon flighting and are recommended for these activities.

Neck

Much depends on the weather and the occasion as to what is appropriate to wear around the neck. Except in a heatwave or when rough-shooting, it is sensible to wear a collar and tie. Although it might seem rather formal, such a combination is extraordinarily effective at keeping the wearer warm in a breeze and reasonably dry in the rain. A checked shirt with a conservative tie is ideal. It is not unknown for a tie to come in useful to secure a splint for a broken limb, be it human or canine.

An item worth carrying in a spare pocket is a towelling cravat. While it could be worn anyway on an informal day, it really comes into its own in wet weather, when it soaks up the rain that would otherwise become an icy trickle down your neck.

Upper Body

A jacket really is the one item not to stint on. On all but the most formal days (and then depending on the weather) the choice is enormous. The very formal day might require a traditional tweed suit comprising jacket, waistcoat, breeches, shooting stockings and stout leather shoes or brogues. It has to be said that such full tweed rig is becoming increasingly rare because in the last few years, developments in protective clothing have been dramatic, not least in improvements to waterproofing and breathability, combined with reductions in weight. At last there are lightweight materials available which perform as well as tweed but which, critically, repel water, unlike tweed which will eventually absorb water however thick or tightly woven it is. Previously, man-made fibres did not keep the wearer warm. To a great degree that has changed although no man-made fibre is ever likely to possess the same degree of heat retention under a wide spectrum of conditions as a natural fibre. Thus, it is now possible to look smart and formal but be more comfortable in extremes of weather.

It is wise to buy the very best that you can afford. Until the early 1990s, the waxed cotton jacket was *de rigueur* for gameshots. Wealthier people also bought expensive waterproof tweed coats with man-made thermal quilted linings and a breathable, waterproof inner membrane, often tailored specifically to the individual. Such coats then became significantly cheaper, often outnumbering waxed cotton jackets at shoots. Wonderfully warm and reasonably resistant to prickly undergrowth, good tweed coats are almost too warm to be worn until well into the shooting season. With the advent of high-tech, lightweight, breathable, waterproof materials which are also warm, the waxed cotton jacket is somewhat obsolete now. Nevertheless, waxed cotton still has one supreme advantage over every other material currently available: it is virtually thornproof and definitely still has a place wherever the wearer might have to push and struggle through thick and prickly cover since even the best 'high-tech' coats are likely to be ripped by brambles.

If there is room only for one shooting coat in your wardrobe, then a 'high-tech' coat would be the one to have, such as the German-made Schoffel jacket; or Barbour's version or one of Musto's products, these latter two being British. For some years, Barbour misguidedly clung to the belief that the waxed cotton jacket would reign supreme for ever. It cost the firm dear but it now makes some very good 'high-tech' breathable, waterproof coats, indeed.

The key criterion when choosing any shooting coat or jacket is that it should be designed for gameshooting, as opposed to clay-pigeon or skeet shooting. It should have plenty of pockets, the main ones strong enough to carry plenty of loose cartridges repeatedly without wearing through, and be loose enough in fit to allow one to swing a gun without feeling any restriction whatsoever. Looseness is important too, to allow additional layers of undergarments to be worn if required. Any shooting coat should be sober in colour, green or brown, and free of bright embellishment, particularly sewn-on badges.

Incidentally, some jackets may be supplied with a belt. For common sense reasons rather than mere snobbery, belts, including cartridge belts, should not be worn outside jackets since they snag easily in undergrowth and prevent the wearer from reaching the inside pockets quickly without having to put down his gun and half-undress in the process. At the same time, a belt also reduces the gap between the inside of the jacket and the next garment and therefore restricts the circulation of warm, insulating air generated by the body. Finally, to nail belts once and for all, they act as tiresome water traps when it is raining.

Underneath

The layer principle should apply when dressing for shooting, on the basis that several thin layers are better than a few thick ones. The aim must be to be comfortable but able to move freely. Encumbrances must be minimized to allow quick and free movement with a gun in the shoulder.

In cold weather, a reasonably thin quilted waistcoat is useful as a thermal lining. Under this, particularly if there is much walking to be done, there should rarely be very much need for more than a lambswool pullover, a shirt and maybe a vest instead of the quilted waistcoat.

In extremely cold conditions or for those with thin blood or bad hangovers, thermal underwear can be beneficial. Thermals, as they are known, should be made from a wool and cotton and/or silk mix, with a small percentage of man-made fibre for strength – they should be thin, light and cellular in construction. It does not necessarily follow that you need to wear both a thermal vest and thermal leggings. A thermal vest should only be necessary if you are likely to be standing for long periods in the sort of conditions that keep polar bears indoors.

Hands

It is extremely dangerous to shoot with hands so cold that they fumble. Gloves, like towelling cravats, should be kept permanently in a recess of one's shooting coat so that they are never left behind. Whether leather or woollen, the trigger finger should be cut away to leave the top two joints free to operate the triggers; most shooting gloves are designed thus these days.

Leather gloves can be a misery in wet weather – slimy and cold – unless they are lined in some way, ideally with a separate silk liner. This is where the woollen glove excels. It is just as warm as leather but, when wet, still keeps the hands warm due to the natural insulating properties of wool. Some woollen gloves have leather sewn into the palms, which aids grip and is recommended. Unfortunately, for all their good qualities, woollen gloves have a depressing propensity to shrink if soaked.

The author also carries a thin pair of silk liner gloves, considering them indispensable. They take up virtually no space and are superb in most conditions until it becomes very cold or wet. Most critically, they are so thin that they enable the wearer to shoot safely without having to expose the trigger finger. Allied to that they are cheap and can be bought from good outdoor clothing retailers.

Legs

Ordinary trousers tucked into wellingtons are fine for dry conditions but act like a drainpipe in the rain by channelling water into the feet of the boots. Breeches are more practical in all conditions – cooler on a hot day and infinitely better in the wet.

Breeches or breeks traditionally used to be styled as plus-fours. These days, plus-fours have largely given way to plus-twos, the number referring to the extra inches required to produce an overhang of material. The overhang is a catchment for any water absorbed by the material and ensures that it drips outside one's boots or not down one's socks if wearing shoes.

As with the rest of the shooting wardrobe, breeches should be loose fitting to allow for easy movement, greater warmth and general comfort, but not excessively so. A good, strong, conservative tweed is recommended since it offers warmth, longevity, smartness and resistance to snagging and precipitation but, once soaked, can be most uncomfortable. Equally practical for informal days are breeches made from moleskin or corduroy, moleskin being far the better of the two.

Lederhosen, as favoured on the Continent, especially in Germany, are good and virtually indestructible – so much so that they are often passed from generation to generation; nevertheless, they look rather (actually, very) out of place in a British shooting environment. Their major failing is that, when soaked, they render walking as easy as walking knee-deep through wet cement; for this reason alone, they are not recommended for wearing in the British climate.

Leggings and Waterproof Trousers Leggings are literally that, consisting of a tube for each leg linked by ties. Trousers are more convenient and offer better protection. Waxed thornproof is good when penetrating thick, wet undergrowth. An alternative might be trousers of rubberised nylon, Gore-tex or similar man-made fibre.

Feet

Shooting socks or stockings should be long enough to provide a generous overlap between their tops and the hems of the breeches. When worn with shoes and therefore exposed to view, they should be restrained in hue and pattern. If hidden inside wellingtons, the colour matters little, within reason, and the extrovert can express himself more or less as he pleases. The best socks are predominantly woollen with a small percentage of man-made fibre to prolong wear. Beware, though, of too thick socks. Ideally a thin inner pair should accompany a thickish pair. If your feet feel too tight in your boots, they will be highly prone to cold because blood flow will be restricted and there will be no air pocket to be warmed by the feet; also, there is an increased risk of getting blisters.

Footwear

In warm, dry conditions, a stout walking boot is recommended since wellingtons make feet sweat. For walking across rugged terrain, it is better to wear walking boots anyway since they afford better ankle support. Puttees with shoes are an alternative, of course, for those with a disposition towards the old-fashioned.

Otherwise, wellingtons are now the most popular footwear. Buy lightweight, green wellingtons which are generally better shaped to the leg, more flexible and comfortable than traditional black ones. There is little to choose between the popular makes. The main disadvantage of wellingtons, as mentioned, is that they cause sweaty feet.

This can be overcome to a large extent by buying oversize boots to allow the comfortable wearing of two pairs of socks. Such a combination absorbs moisture, keeps the feet dry and provides good insulation in cold conditions. As with everything else, it is possible to be extravagant and go for a leather-lined 'super welly' which can even, in extremis, be tailored to fit the leg. They are outstandingly comfortable but cost five or six times more than more conventional wellingtons. By virtue of their leather lining, sweaty feet are almost eliminated. Inevitably, there is a disadvantage in that, sooner or later, the leather lining will rot due to the cumulative effects of sweat; on balance, the author feels that they are an unnecessary extravagance.

Increasingly popular are fully waterproof, breathable all leather calf-length boots. All versions are expensive but universally comfortable and practical, fully living up to their makers' claims. It is recommended that such boots are not worn in very hot weather or for long walks, particularly across rugged terrain, since proper walking boots are much more suitable, offering better support.

EQUIPMENT

Theoretically, once equipped, the game shot should be set up for life. There should be no need to replace the essentials or hardwear items of his inventory, such as guns and cartridge bags, unless he succumbs to self-indulgence or used a false economy in the first place. Like any interest though, there is never a dearth of new gadgets, which once bought, become instantly indispensable. Self-restraint should be the novice's maxim: it is idiotic to spend a small fortune only to decide that you dislike shooting after one day's shooting.

GAMESHOOTER'S ESSENTIAL EQUIPMENT

The list of equipment is in alphabetical order and annotated:

E – Essential

D – Desirable/Useful

L – Luxury

Cartridges (E) Buy the best you can afford. The cheapest cartridges can represent a false economy and are more likely to perform less effectively. Certainly, cartridges of British origin are pretty satisfactory but some are more satisfactory than others and almost invariably these are the most expensive ones. There is a surprising difference in the performance of cartridges. Experienced guns have their own preferences but the novice should seek advice from a gunshop.

Cartridge Bag (E) A cartridge bag full of cartridges will be adequate for most days and is a convenient way of carrying up to 100 cartridges, bearing in mind that 50 may be comfortable to carry but 100 is another matter altogether. Many Guns put enough cartridges in a pocket until they are likely to meet up with their cartridge bag again, rather than lugging the whole lot from drive to drive; not easy if towing a dog, carrying a gun and sundry other impedimenta nor a good idea on a day where one could use several pocketfuls of cartridges on each drive. Only buy leather or canvas bags since plastic ones do not last, retain moisture and nor do they breathe, which is anathema to cartridges.

It is sensible to buy a bag with a canvas shoulder strap rather than a leather strap, which adds to the weight, particularly if wet, and is less comfortable than canvas. It is wise, too, to have your initials embossed on the oval part of the securing strap on the flap of the bag, for easy recognition among several other bags in the back of a trailer, Land Rover or whatever other shoot transport is provided. Another means of identification is to have a saddler replace the canvas strap with a distinctive one of your own; regimental stable belts are a perfect substitute, for example.

Cartridge Belt (E) If worn, a cartridge belt is usually worn under a jacket unless rough-shooting – apart from anything else, this protects the cartridges from the elements and eliminates the tell-tale reflection from their bases. A cartridge belt provides a handy reserve – it is impossible to predict cartridge expenditure and twenty-five cartridges (the average contents of a box and capacity of the average belt) is a very useful reserve for unexpected quantities of birds.

A belt should be leather with a wide strap to allow for extra layers of clothing or seasonal over-indulgence. Closed loops are better than open loops since cartridges cannot slip through accidentally.

Cartridge Magazine (L) A cartridge magazine looks like a small suitcase or attache case with compartments. Although heavy, they enable one to keep cartridges with different loads or shot size separately, i.e. heavier loads for duck flighting with No. 4 or 5 and No. 6, No. 7, etc. for game shooting. Different calibre cartridges, e.g. 12 and 20 bore, *should not* be carried in the same magazine under any circumstances, though. They are only really useful for a two-gun day with loaders, since they allow quicker access to cartridges when reloading, and are the most effective way to carry large numbers of cartridges. The average magazine holds 250.

Cleaning Kit (E) Do not stint on your cleaning kit – cheap cleaning rods could result in barrels scored irreparably by badly-finished fittings. Most cleaning kits containing rods, phosphor bronze brush, sheepskin brush or wool mop, pull-through, patches and oil, cost a few pounds only; obviously each item is available individually.

A very effective and most highly recommended additional item is a Paradox cleaning rod. This is a rod enveloped in washable nylon fur which is quite remarkable in the way that it removes the heaviest deposits; also, it has the advantage that it is virtually impossible to scratch the barrels in any way with it.

First Aid Kit (E) An item carried by relatively few people, it is not so much for humans as for dogs which injure themselves on wire or other sharp objects. Ensure that a first aid kit is kept in the car and includes antiseptic cream (Savlon or similar) and cotton wool in addition to the standard and often basic items provided.

Game Bag (D) An essential item for the rough shooter likely to kill a lot of game, or for walking Guns unaccompanied by armies of beaters. Traditional game bags are canvas with a net pouch on the outside, a strong plastic lining and a wide canvas shoulder strap. A game bag is not required for driven shoots.

Game Book (D) A game book is a historical record of a sportsman's shooting career, showing where and when he shot what with whom, plus a brief description of each day. It should not be treated as merely a tally to be added to at every opportunity. Be wary of making personal comments, if there is any likelihood of somebody else reading it!

Guns (E) Countless volumes are available already on the subject of guns. Nevertheless, it is so important that it is necessary to devote more than just passing comment to the matter.

Type It is essential to buy the right gun for the right occasion. In the same way that a table tennis bat is unsuitable for tennis, so a pump-gun is inappropriate for a formal, driven pheasant shoot. A side-by-side shotgun will not be out of place on any occasion, whether it be a game or clay pigeon shoot. Today the old prejudice against over-and-unders is rarely encountered and they now outsell side-by-sides. Interestingly, many regular grouse shots actually favour lightweight over-and-unders, and then revert to side-by-sides for pheasant.

Over-and-unders, however, can be heavier to carry and more awkward to hold and quickly reload than conventional side-by-side guns.

If buying second-hand, avoid hammer guns which demand even higher standards of care and alertness from the user. Hammer guns started to go out of fashion at the beginning of the twentieth century but are still available.

Bore Size The majority of gameshots use 12 bores, although 16 bores are usually lighter and nearly as effective, while 20 bores are lighter still.
Weight takes on greater significance with advancing years. The key advantage of a 12 bore is that it can fire a heavier charge of shot, something which is more important if wildfowling, for example. Also, in an emergency, you are likely to be able to buy or borrow 12 bore cartridges more readily than any other size.

Make Some of the best shotguns are made in Great Britain as, indeed, are some of the most expensive. Other countries, particularly Spain and Italy, make extremely good guns which, while cheaper and not sharing the same cachet as English guns, could last an owner's and his children's lifetimes, with care. If you can possibly afford it, buy a gun with ejectors; a gun without them is a real hindrance on a busy drive.

Cost 'You gets what you pays for' holds very true when buying a gun. Today, depending on the engraving, it is possible to pay £90,000+ for a new Purdey or Holland and Holland, to name but two of the best makers (many people buy them in pairs, incidentally). A made-to-measure English boxlock costs about £15,000+. A Spanish AYA sidelock costs between £3,000 and £10,000 and an AYA boxlock, depending on embellishment, between £1,000 and £4,000. It is possible to pay as little as £400 for a side-by-side but 'You gets what you pays for...' Buy the best you can afford.

Safety It is an offence to use, sell or offer for sale a gun that is out of proof or unsafe in any way. Unless buying from a reputable dealer or maker, it is essential to seek the advice of a professional gunsmith before paying for a gun.

Fitment If a gun does not fit, it could result in consistently poor shooting. Even an eighth of an inch too much or too little in the stock can make all the difference. Most gunsmiths can alter stocks easily but not while you wait. Incidentally, when being measured, wear your normal shooting jacket.

Gun Cabinet (E) Gun cabinets will certainly become a legal requirement as part of owning a gun; currently they are not under the *Firearms (Amendment) Act 1988*, even though most police forces insist now that private firearms must now be kept in them. If that is not the case, the police will still be more inclined to issue a shotgun certificate if they know a gun will be secured in a cabinet. Cabinets can also be wired in to burglar alarm systems. A cabinet should be secured to the wall and floor or else it could easily be stolen with its contents. As already stressed, avoid locating a gun cabinet in an area prone to dampness such as a cellar.

There is no particular brand which stands out; buy the strongest you can afford and one which meets minimum recommended police standards – these include concealed hinges which cannot be tampered with, double 5 lever locks and at least 14 gauge steel construction. While not always feasible – and some cabinet manufacturers make a point of including ammunition storage space – try to avoid storing ammunition in the same place as guns. Bear in mind the over-riding police stipulation that guns must be kept in a secure manner; a gun cabinet virtually obviates the problem.

Gun Case (D/E) A gun case is useful if transporting a gun a long distance in a full car and essential if going by air or sea. Otherwise, it is usually adequate to carry a gun in a car in a gun sleeve. It is ludicrous to spend a fortune on a gun and then not keep it carefully when travelling. Gun cases range from the moulded plastic variety to hand-made leather and oak. Plastic cases are more easily damaged, whereas leather-covered wooden cases tend to be able to take remarkable battering but are quite heavy. Virtually all gun cases have compartments for cleaning equipment.

Gun Sleeve (E) If a shoot involves much getting into and out of vehicles, a sleeve (sometimes called a slip or cover) is recommended to reduce the chances of damage to the gun; it also saves walking about with an open gun and virtually eliminates the chance of an accidental discharge. In fact it is foolish not to use a gun sleeve and, indeed, some shoots now insist on them being used. Try to avoid plastic sleeves since they prevent air circulating, thereby encouraging rust and rot in damp conditions. Fleece-lined leather covers are nice but expensive. A lined, heavy-duty canvas or waxed cotton sleeve is very adequate. Whether you buy a sleeve with a full length zip or a flap at the stock end is a matter of preference. Zips can be awkward if wet, rusty or damaged and render the sleeve utterly useless if so, whereas the flap type can be more easily mended *in situ*.

Never store a gun in its sleeve since the risk of damage from moisture is very serious, whatever material the sleeve is made from. Always dry a sleeve after use, especially if there has been moisture about.

Heat/Hand Guards (L) These slide over the barrels of a side-by-side to protect the leading hand from blistering on hot barrels. They are necessary mainly when firing a lot of cartridges in rapid succession, such as during a shooting lesson or for large-bag days which do not warrant two guns per person. Alternatively, and to some extent more effective, a woollen glove may be used.

Knife (E) You might never need it but you will be enormously grateful you carried one should you have cause to use it. A small, sharp, wooden-handled, French Opinel pocket-knife is ideal. These knives are cheap, very sharp and versatile enough to gralloch a deer in emergency – the author once had to do this when he came across a severely injured deer on a pheasant shoot and was most grateful for his knife – or to administer the picnic. The law now states that it is illegal to carry a knife in a public place without good reason or lawful authority. A public place is anywhere to which the public has access. This not only covers areas such as public footpaths, but also estate land where the public may have access even if it is privately owned. Your car or other vehicle is also classed as a public place whilst on the highway, and the police now have search and seize powers without warrant with respect to knives.

Shooters and stalkers can show 'good reason' for carrying a knife if they have reasonable grounds for expecting to need it while pursuing a lawful activity. This would cover you on the shoot and travelling to or from it but not at any other time.

There is an exemption in law for folding pocket knives with a cutting edge of less than three inches, but it must be foldable at all times, so knives such as Opinel, which use a manual twist collar to hold the blade in the open position, are termed to be lock knives for which you need a 'good reason'.

Leather Protector (D) It is possible to buy canvas ones. The author makes his own from scrap leather, as described on page 25.

Shooting Stick (D) Not really necessary unless you are slightly infirm or injured, and expecting to be a long time waiting at stands, especially when shooting grouse. Something of a nuisance to carry if already encumbered by gun, game and dog, but it is possible to buy a very neat folding 'flip' stick which is light, strong and easily portable.

Stick (D/E) A stick with a shaped horn or bone handle which should be roughly long enough to rest against the biceps. Useful for support across tricky terrain and for tethering a dog to.

Torch (E) Essential only really if wildfowling or duck-flighting. These days there are several small but impressively efficient torches about, especially the little steel-bodied ones, which can double as a 'priest'. Whatever you buy, ensure it is waterproof.

Whistle (E) Only essential for dog owners and wildfowlers. A whistle (unless it is of the dubiously useful 'Silent' type) is more likely to carry further than the voice, which could make all the difference to a wildfowler trapped in mud. 'ACME Thunderers', and police whistles should be avoided, since they are too intrusive or likely to be used by keepers and shoot captains on occasion, to indicate the start and finish of drives. Hand-made bone whistles, for example, are ideal, each having its own unique tone which will not result in a plethora of confused dogs when blown.

Wristwatch (E) This is mentioned in the very unlikely event that somebody might not carry one. Apart from anything else, a watch is essential as an aid to arriving at a shoot on time; it is unforgivable to arrive late at a shoot. Unlike most other social events, it is essential to turn up early to a shoot so as not to ruin the host's carefully-laid plans. A watch is equally essential for the foreshore wildfowler to keep abreast of the tidal situation, since in the dark it is very difficult to know what the state of the tide is.

Conclusion

This chapter has attempted to give a balanced ideal of what is safe to wear in the shooting field. False economy could cost life. In the case of clothing, the loss of life would probably be confined to the wearer. This may sound alarmist but it is true, especially for the wildfowler.

The effects of errors in one's choice of attire may only manifest themselves years later through rheumatism and arthritis. It is sensible therefore to look after oneself and never take the weather for granted. Whatever the case, if you look after yourself it will go some way to making you a safer shot.

7

GUNDOGS

This chapter offers broad advice only. Each heading warrants a separate book. When one considers how little a dog costs, in relative terms, and how much it does for its owner, it offers the best value for money imaginable; that is, as long as its master shows and tells it exactly what is required of it. So often, dogs are expected to be clairvoyant as to their masters' demands and are berated for inevitably failing. Ultimately, a dog can only be as good as its handler/master.

WHICH BREED?

Gundogs fulfil three roles: finding game, flushing it and retrieving when it has been shot. Most dogs can combine two and often all three of these roles but their strength usually lies in one particular aspect of the job. If your interest is mainly in driven shooting, you will probably prefer a labrador that waits patiently at the peg but can retirieve the longest runner. If you spend more time beating and rough shooting, a spaniel that can hunt, flush and retrieve all day may be a better choice. But provided you are aware of the limitations, the best choice is the dog you feel comfortable with, and that feels comfortable with you.

Unless you are an expert in a particular breed, it may be wise to avoid rarer, more exotic breeds of gundog. Rare breeds are more likely to be inbred, highly-strung, prone to genetic failings, difficult to handle and unpredictable towards other people.

Points to Look For

When choosing any dog, look for a combination of the following: fearlessness; its reaction to sudden noise i.e. is it likely to be gun-shy?; good coat; straight legs; broad head; good wagging tail; bright eyes and friendly disposition. Avoid: over-excited dogs; timidity; dogs with very pale eyes (this is the author's prejudice since it often seems to indicate a shifty, potentially aggressive, untrustworthy animal, but is not a hard and fast rule); in-breeding (look at the pedigree). Follow your instincts, since you will almost immediately sense whether an animal may be right or wrong. Gundogs can suffer from hereditary conditions such as retinitis and hip dysplasia, so ask for evidence that the parents have been screened for this.

WORKING STRAIN

If going for a pedigree dog, make sure it is bred from working stock and not show stock. A Crufts champion is bred for showing and may well cringe at the mere mention of shooting. A study of a dog's pedigree will reveal the right signs by the prefixes FTCh (Field Trial Champion) and FTW (Field Trial Winner) in front of the Kennel Name, e.g. FTCh Victrix of Shermill. There is little doubt that dogs inherit skills or aptitudes. Thus a long line of FTChs is a good indicator of inherent ability; it is far from a guarantee though.

Since dogs bred for trialling are often too hot to handle for the non-expert, buying a dog from a gamekeeper will usually produce a reliable working dog and you should be able to see the parents working, which is a good indication of the pup's potential.

Labrador

For elegance, reliability and general-purposefulness, I think a labrador has no peer, although a golden retriever runs it fairly close. The main qualities of a labrador are: friendliness, loyalty, athleticism, ease to train, strength, hardiness, stamina, adaptability, steadiness, intelligence, trustworthiness with children and a desire to please. Conversely, a labrador is fairly large, more circumspect about diving into just any piece of cover, often a scavenger, and less likely to work flat out all day on a rough shoot without a tailing-off in performance.

Spaniel

By and large, gameshooters in Great Britain either have labradors or spaniels. The debate over their relative merits is never likely to diminish in its intensity. Spaniels' good qualities are: an ability to work flat out all day without respite, boundless energy, compactness and therefore better ability to work thick cover, nimbleness, agility and friendliness. Their minus points are, and remember these are generalizations and not necessarily applicable to every single dog: excitability; ability to attract dirt, burrs and foreign bodies, especially in and around their ears; greater resistance to training; and need for greater discipline.

If a gun dog becomes ill-disciplined, it can be redeemed only with difficulty in the case of the labrador, whereas a spaniel is almost impossible to bring back to its peak.

Golden Retriever

Golden retrievers are very similar to labradors in almost all respects. The only significant difference is that golden retrievers have long coats and, like spaniels, tend to attract every burr and twig within a ten-foot radius of action.

Flatcoat Retriever

Flatcoats are black and long-coated. While they have most of the characteristics of labradors and retrievers, they tend to be more excitable and challenging to control. By way of categorisation, flatcoats fall somewhere between labradors and spaniels in temperament. They are usually brilliant in water.

English Pointer and English, Irish or Gordon Setter

These breeds are not really suited to driven shooting. They are bred to work on grouse moors and have limited use in enclosed country, particularly since they no longer retrieve. Prospective buyers should seek guidance and advice, possibly from the National Gundog Association. These breeds tend to be fairly highly-strung, pointers being more wary of strangers and less predictable in their behaviour, whereas setters are very friendly (and sloppy).

Dog or Bitch?

Some people say that bitches are more placid, more steady and more loyal than dogs. This is an erroneous generalization since the key lies with the owner and how he or she handles the animal.

In the simplest terms, bitches come into season twice a year, of which once will always coincide with the shooting season. Since it is very bad form to take a bitch in season shooting – because it completely destroys the concentration of all male dogs present – this means being without a dog for at least two weeks. Of course, a bitch can be spayed, a process that can render – but not always – a bitch permanently 'interesting' to other dogs. This is unfortunate since the innocent owner will have to suffer thinly veiled sneers as much as if his bitch really was in season: 'It's damned irresponsible to bring a bitch in season, etc. etc... ' A good bitch can be a lucrative source of income in terms of breeding potential, though; but, if choosing a gundog, this should not be a first priority.

Dogs do not suffer from the same problems but may be less steady. Once indoctrinated in the ways of the birds and bees, there is a danger that they will try to roam. They can earn money through stud fees. Although the income will only equate to the cost of one pup from the resultant litter, there is not the attendant inconvenience of raising and selling a whole litter.

Breeding Etiquette

It is worth mentioning a few points of etiquette concerning the breeding of dogs. It is customary to take the bitch to the dog, since it is the bitch owner's responsibility to seek a mate. One advantage of so doing is that the dog is less likely to develop a roaming instinct; the theory being that he will not think he has to travel in search of satisfaction. The dog owner's payment is either the same as the selling price of one pup or pick of the litter. Litters from two pedigree, Kennel Club-registered dogs should be registered immediately; this makes the pups more valuable which, in turn, will apply to their progeny. In addition, the Kennel Club will require a hip and eye score certificate from a vet.

Whatever the choice of breed and sex, a dog is only as good as its master. If a dog does not work for you, it is unlikely that any other dog will; miracles are not common in this sphere. True, a poor or even rogue animal could be the cause, but real rogues are relatively rare. Whatever the case, before condemning a dog as useless, ask an expert to try their hand with it first.

CARE OF DOGS WHEN SHOOTING

So many owners, the author being no exception, tend to take their dogs too much for granted. The points that follow may go some way towards redressing the situation.

EQUIPMENT FOR THE GAMESHOOTER'S DOG

Regardless of the weather forecast, always assume the worst will happen and that, even if it does not rain, your dog will find some way of drenching itself, usually towards the end of the last drive. With this criterion in mind, you should be able to plan your dog's needs by covering every eventuality at little inconvenience to yourself and considerable benefit to your dog. Items to include are:

- *Lead*
- *Whistle*
- *Tether – if necessary*
- *Bed – if a long journey is entailed*
- *Towelling blanket (see the Duck-flighting drive in Chapter 1, page 31) or bag, or at least a towel*
- *Snack for lunch – a few biscuits*
- *Evening meal – if a long journey is entailed*
- *Dog bowl – in the event of a meal being necessary*
- *Water bowl and bottle of water*
- *First Aid Kit – see page 82*

WHAT A DOG MIGHT EXPECT FROM HIS MASTER DURING THE SHOOTING DAY

A dog's demands are not onerous, when one considers what the dog does in return. From a dog's point of view, it would be reasonable to expect his master to do the following, as the day progresses:

- Remember to take the dog.
- Provide breakfast if there will be a lot of work to do, assuming that the dog does not usually have breakfast.*
- Remember to load all his kit (the dog's) in the car.
- Not let the dog attempt anything foolish, such as jumping high barbed wire fences, or over-extending himself. If you have one, use a leather protector when appropriate.
- Inspect for thorns and injuries at lunch.
- At lunch, provide a few biscuits and water if none have been available previously.
- Inspect for thorns, etc. before going home.
- If wet, either put into a towelling bag or rub with a towel. Dogs are just as prone as humans to the vagaries of rheumatism and arthritis.
- If a long journey means a late return, the dog should be fed, otherwise feed on return home.
- A final check for thorns and injuries, once home.
- Remember to take your dog home – it is surprisingly easy to fail to notice your dog is not in your car in your haste to get home, especially if it has leapt into somebody else's vehicle.

---

* This pre-supposes that most owners feed their dogs their main meal in the evenings which, obviously, is not always the case. It is important not to disrupt the dog's feeding pattern.

8

TREATMENT OF GAME

Having shot one's quarry it is necessary to know how to dispatch it, carry it, hang it and prepare it for the table. Often the hunter's responsibilities stop there. Thus this chapter makes no mention of cooking, except to mention two definitive game cookery books, which are: *The Game Cookbook* by Clarissa Dickson Wright and *The Poacher's Cookbook* by Prue Coats.

Dispatch

Always dispatch wounded game as soon as possible, with the minimum of suffering. If game has suffered unnecessary trauma before dying, it can lend a bitter flavour to the meat sometimes. With practice, a sharp knock on the back of the head is the quickest and most effective method, irrespective of species.

FEATHERED GAME

With feathered game, either: hold the bird firmly in both hands with the breast uppermost and strike its head hard against a hard surface such as a tree, stone or fence post; or hold the bird by the neck in one hand and strike the back of its head firmly with a stick, taking care not to kill your fingers. Alternatively, and less dangerous, clutch small species (**partridge, grouse, woodcock** and **snipe**) around the body and hit the head sharply against your stick. To test whether the bird, and indeed any species, is dead or not, breathe on or touch an eye, which should appear dull and glazed but, more obviously, should not blink if the creature is dead.

It is possible, as another option, with young **grouse** and smaller species (**partridge, snipe, woodcock**), to kill them by crushing their skulls. The technique is to hold the bird by the neck between forefinger and second finger, and squeeze down with your thumb on the top of the skull until you feel it break inwards. This is a rapid and easy means of dispatch but, if inexperienced, do avoid protracting the process, indeed, use another method altogether.

With practice, it is possible to kill a **pheasant** by a deft and not over-exuberant twist of the neck, holding the bird by the head and using a combination of a quick flick and twist. This is not suitable for other species, particularly grouse, partridge and pigeon, since the head is apt to part company with the body with astonishing ease. On the other hand, it is exceptionally difficult to wring a duck's neck but again, with practice, a deft twist and flick will be effective. It is well-nigh impossible, though, to wring the neck of a goose, which has a neck of inordinate elasticity, and it should not be attempted. Quite apart from the suffering that will be caused, the birds are likely to be grossly disfigured.

Another method is to use a Priest, which is a short (6") cosh, normally used by fishermen. If there is still room in your pockets, then it might be a most useful device.

If lucky enough to pick a snipe or woodcock, remove the legs beneath the 'knees' immediately, while still warm and before *rigor mortis* renders the operation much harder and probably impossible. The technique is to hold the thigh firmly between forefinger and thumb, hold the lower limb, break it and twist the lower limb for several turns, simultaneously pulling firmly. After some resistance, the lower leg should come away along with the tendons, which are like slivers of bone if left for cooking. The result of this action will be that each thigh can be eaten whole less the single thigh bone in the middle; otherwise, woodcock and snipe legs are hardly worth the effort since they are so bony or, more accurately, sinewy. This technique may be used at the plucking stage with duck, grouse and partridge. The undamaged legs of a woodcock are exquisite and more than justify the effort in removing the sinews.

GROUND GAME

Rabbits and hares may be dispatched identically. While they too can be killed by a sharp knock on the head as described, this method is neither necessary nor recommended. Take either species by both hind legs, holding upside-down firmly in your non-master hand. With the master hand, administer a sharp, downwards, karate-style chop to the back of the neck. You will only hurt your hand if you fail to use sufficient determination in what is a surprisingly simple procedure. Hares, when wounded, scream in the most heart-rending, pathetic fashion; do not be deterred but, rather, use this as an incentive to dispatch the beast as quickly as possible. Once either species is dead, hold the animal tail downwards in both hands, squeezing progressively on the abdomen to evacuate the bladder, which will otherwise do so where you would prefer it did not, later on.

Rabbits should be paunched (gutted) on arrival at home. Many people do the same with hares, although others prefer them hung intact for a few days. If you are rash enough to shoot a hare a long way from home on a rough or walked-up shoot, it is customary to carry it yourself.

SOME DO'S AND DON'TS

- **DON'T** shoot wounded quarry, except for strongly running hares and rabbits and then only if it is safe to do so. Apart from the fact that it is dangerous to shoot at close quarters, particularly because of the risk from ricochets, the quarry is likely to be destroyed or rendered useless for eating.

- **DO** note the birds you have hit on a driven shoot and check with a picker-up that they have been collected.

- **DO** make every reasonable effort to find wounded game but temper this with common sense, and don't delay the next drive too long lest you disrupt the whole day's programme, for which your host will certainly not thank you. On a driven shoot, wounded game may well be picked by a picker-up or by the keeper the day after a shoot. Regardless, it is essential to inform one's host of the assessed whereabouts of an unpicked wounded bird.

- **DO** try to get a dog to seek out wounded game but don't let it, or indeed yourself, chase a runner into the next drive's covert since it will most certainly ruin that drive by disturbing the game in it. If in doubt, check with the host or keeper before sending your dog in.

CARRIAGE OF GAME

In principle, game should be carried the same way up that it will be hung at home. Thus, feathered game should be carried by the neck, head uppermost, while rabbits and hares should be carried by the hind legs, head at the bottom. (At times, on the Continent, some smaller game birds are hung by the feet). With rabbits and hares, convenience dictates the method of carriage as much as anything else... if in doubt, try carrying them head uppermost to see what I mean.

For the journey home after a shoot, there is no harm in placing game on its side, although for a journey of several hours in a probably warm car, game should be hung. Unless you trust your dog implicitly, it is as well not to put your game where the dog can feast himself, nor is it fair to do so.

HANGING GAME

Without going into a biological dissertation as to why game should hang and not lie on its side, suffice it to say that game on its side decomposes beyond the edible very quickly. With most species, hanging positively improves the flavour. If you think chicken is bland, it is exquisite compared to a pheasant that has not been hung at all. Some people maintain that hanging makes old birds less tough. While there may be some truth in this, in reality this theory is only true if the bird is hung to the point of decomposition; it is the method of cooking that is critical.

While it is convenient to hang birds in pairs, if you have space try to hang birds individually. Simply tie a noose of string with a slip knot around one bird and do the same with the other end of the string round the second bird. Then hang them over a nail or hook. With rabbits and hares, cut a slit in one hind leg, right through between the bone and tendon above the bottom joint, force the other leg through the slit and then hang over a hook. The more air circulation there is around hanging game the better.

Hang game unplucked with stomach intact, in a cool, well-ventilated, shaded place protected from predators such as pets and especially cats. A garage is often the nearest solution available but should be made cat-proof, i.e. keep the doors closed. Everybody has their own ideas on length of hanging; in essence, it depends very much on the weather, on the species, and on personal taste. If the body comes away from the head, it may be safe to say that the game is overhung!

The following minimum times are fairly conservative since the author prefers his game to be not too gamey:

SUGGESTED HANGING TIMES BY SPECIES

Species	Minimum (more applicable early season)	Maximum (more applicable late season)
Grouse	1 day	7 days
Ptarmigan	1 day	7 days
Partridge	2/3 days	7 days
Pheasant	4 days	10/12 days
Duck	1 day	3 days
Woodcock	1 day	3 days
Snipe	1 day	3 days
Pigeon	1 day	3 days
Hare	4 days	10 days
Rabbit	1 day	3 days
Goose	3 days	10 days

NB. In very mild weather, these times could be halved, particularly with duck and geese.

PLUCKING

The longer they hang, the harder birds are to pluck without tearing the skin. There are many ways to pluck a bird and only experience can really provide the best method. To some extent, it is true to say that the larger the bird, the harder it is to pluck. Incidentally, the same principles apply to all birds except pigeons. Pigeons differ in that, while they can be treated as any other species, it is equally simple to pluck the breasts, and then cut them off, discarding the rest, including the skin from each breast.

Two methods of plucking:

1. (especially for small birds) Put an open, large capacity supermarket carrier bag in a sink and have to hand a pair of good quality game shears/scissors; failing the shears, a robust, sharp knife will suffice. Remove the legs immediately above the knee, leaving the thigh intact. With duck, grouse and partridge it is worth removing the tendons as described for woodcock and snipe. Unlike woodcock and snipe which ideally need to have their tendons removed while still warm, duck, grouse and partridge can wait until the plucking stage. Remove the wings at the first joint of the wing. Removal of these extremities makes the bird more manageable and saves unnecessary plucking.

Now work to a sequence. For example, pluck the tail feathers first, then the legs, then the back, finishing with the breast or underside, which is the most fiddly bit and where the skin is most likely to rip. To reduce the risk of tearing the skin, take a few feathers at a time between finger and thumb, as near their base as possible, holding the bird on the draining board firmly in the other hand with its head furthest away from you. Tease the feathers gently in the direction of the head, putting the feathers in the carrier bag. Try to get into the habit of pressing against the flesh around the area being plucked at the same time as plucking or else you will tear the skin very easily.

Once you reach the neck, pluck just enough feathers so that when you decapitate the bird you do not remove any breast. Cut off the head and neck as near the breast as possible and discard. With grouse, pheasants, geese, duck and partridges, press gently on the centre of the breast bone to evacuate the crop of its contents – recently fed pheasants' crops will contain corn while grouse's will contain heather. Turn the bird round and make no longer than an inch-long incision in the underside of the anus with the shears. Insert one finger and remove the innards before rinsing through under cold water. The squeamish may prefer to don rubber gloves prior to this last operation. Please note that quail and snipe are not worth gutting and are best cooked with their innards *in situ*; some like their woodcock this way. With a pheasant, this whole process will take anything between ten and thirty minutes depending on experience.

Put all the feathers, extremities and gory bits in the carrier bag and throw in the dustbin. Responsibility for the bird may then be entrusted to the cook.

It is worth singling out duck. Duck have a mass of fluffy down, close to their skin, which is a nuisance to pluck. When you have tired of removing the down and are left with a few wisps, rub the flesh vigorously, which removes most downy residue very effectively.

2. (especially for large birds) The following method really only applies to geese, mallard or pheasants, everything else being small enough to comfortably hold in one hand. Hold the bird firmly and pluck the feathers from both sides of the wings, close to the body, before cutting off the two outer sections of the wings.

Tie the bird's feet together and hang on a convenient nail or hook over a sack or dustbin, inside an outhouse or garage; feathers will blow all over the place outside. Also, unless your outhouse is heated, this method, late in the season, is recommended only for the hardiest sportsman.

Pluck downwards, towards the head, using the same plucking technique as the first method described. Once plucked, remove the legs and head and gut as before.

SKINNING

The process of skinning and gutting hares and rabbits is more or less identical for each species.

Lay the animal on its back. Make a shallow incision with a sharp knife between the forelegs and continue the cut down to the hind legs. The cut should be shallow enough to cut the skin but not penetrate into the stomach. Grip the skin either side of the incision and gently pull apart to expose the stomach. Turn the animal over. Hold the head and hind legs and very sharply flick the body down, this should eject the stomach. Cut the connections at either end, releasing the stomach, and then remove any other internal organs which may still be attached.

Remove the feet, then gently prise the skin from around the body as much as possible so that only the head and legs are covered. Bend the body backwards to enable the hind legs to be pulled out of the skin, possibly applying the knife around the tall. Pull the skin towards the head, over the forelegs, thus leaving the skin attached to the head. Cut off the head, close to the shoulders. Once again, the point has been reached where the cook assumes command.

It seems to be increasingly popular to skin pheasants, remove the breasts and discard the rest of the carcass. The technique is to cut through the vent, through the feathers and skin, up to the base of the neck. Peel back the skin over the breasts and carefully cut them off. You can also peel the thighs and legs using game shears to detach them from the remaining carcass.

9

THE LAW

This chapter gives an outline of the current situation in England, Wales and Scotland. In Northern Ireland, different laws apply and they are currently under review.

While the contents of this chapter are published in good faith and the advice is correct at the time of going to press, it is not an official authority. To that end it may be treated only as a guide and neither the author nor publisher can accept liability for advice that may be rendered erroneous should the law change regarding Firearms and Shotguns. This section draws on:

Guide of Firearms Licensing Law 2013, on the Home Office website.

Game Licences

Game licences in England, Scotland, Wales and Northern Ireland have been abolished.

Shotgun Certificates

There is no lower age restriction on the possession of a shotgun certificate - the author's son had one aged 10. It is a wise precaution to have one to avoid any assertion of illegality, should a child receive an invitation to shoot over somebody else's land. Without a shotgun certificate, it is illegal to use a shotgun unless the gun belongs to the occupier of the land over which the shoot is taking place and is used in the occupier's presence.

Borrowed Shotguns

An individual not in possession of a shotgun certificate may borrow a shotgun from the owner or occupier of private land or premises and use it in their presence. If under 15, the individual must be supervised by a person aged 21 or over. 'Occupier' generally means anyone with any right to hunt, fish, shoot or take game. In 'the presence of' is taken to mean in sight and/or earshot.

THE PURCHASE, POSSESSION AND USE OF SHOT GUNS BY JUNIORS

Under 15

It is an offence to make a gift of a shotgun or ammunition to a person under 15 years old. A person may not have an assembled shotgun with him except:

    I. When he is under the direct supervision of someone aged 21 or over, in which case, providing he has a valid shotgun certificate, he may use the shotgun under that person's instruction, or

    2. When the shotgun is in a securely fastened gun cover so that it cannot be fired.

Age 15 to 17

A person between the ages of 15 and 17 may be given or lent a shotgun and ammunition but he may not buy them.

After reaching the age of 15, a person may use a shotgun without supervision, providing he holds a valid shotgun certificate.

GUNS THAT NEED A SHOTGUN CERTIFICATE

A shotgun is a smooth-bored gun which meets all the following criteria:

1. has a barrel length of not less that 24" , and a bore of 2" or less in diameter;

2. does not have a magazine, or has a non-detachable magazine which cannot hold more than two cartridges; and

3. is not a revolver (i.e. a gun containing a series of chambers which revolve when the gun is fired).

Where a gun's magazine has been adapted to hold no more than two cartridges, rather than being constructed from new in this way, it must be certified as such by the London or Birmingham Proof Houses.

SECURE STORAGE

General Principles

A shotgun certificate will specify the description of the shotguns to which it relates. This will include, where known, the identification numbers of the guns. The Firearms Rules 2013 state that as a prescribed condition of a certificate, 'Firearms and shotguns to which this certificate relates must be stored securely at all times (except in certain circumstances) so as to prevent, so far as is reasonably practicable, access to the guns by unauthorised persons'. The Rules do NOT prescribe the form of safekeeping or security but it is expected that guns will be kept in a purpose-built gun cabinet and the police may try to insist on this although it is not a legal requirement.

Transporting Shotguns and Ammunition

Guns and ammunition should be hidden from view, preferably in a locked boot. If you leave a gun in an unattended vehicle, remove the fore-end. Whenever practicable, guns and ammunition should not be stored together in a vehicle. Also if practicable, ammunition should be secured in an appropriate container, ideally secured to the vehicle. It is possible to buy means of securing guns to a vehicle's structure using cables, clamps or security cases.

PURCHASE OF AMMUNITION

If you buy ammunition (a cartridge containing five or more pellets none of which exceeds .360" in diameter – LG shot or 000 Buckshot), you must produce the appropriate firearms or shotgun certificate, or written authority from a certificate holder, authorising you to buy it, together with the holder's original certificate. The only exception to this is ammunition that is subject to control under Sections 1 or 5 of the Firearms Act 1968.

SHOTGUNS – A GUIDE TO THE LAW

Applying for a Shotgun Certificate

You should apply for a shotgun certificate to the firearms licensing department of the police force in whose area you are living. Instructions for completing the application form are necessarily thorough but straightforward to understand. Shotgun certificates contain a 45mm x 35mm passport-sized photograph of the holder, a detailed description of all guns held on the certificate, including any identification numbers if known. You will therefore need to provide this information on the shotgun certificate application form. Safekeeping conditions appear on all shotgun certificates. This creates two distinct levels of security to ensure safe custody of the guns.

Criteria for the Issue of a Shotgun Certificate

A chief officer of police may refuse to grant a shotgun certificate if:

1. He is not satisfied that the applicant can possess a shotgun without danger to public safety or to the peace.

2. The applicant does not have to make out a case for wishing to possess shotguns; neither does he have to give good reason for possessing one.

Common Expiry Dates for Shotgun and Firearms Certificates

A firearm certificate holder applying for the granting or renewal of a shotgun certificate can ask for it to be issued with the same expiry date as his firearm certificate. Alternatively, where a shotgun certificate holder applies for the grant or renewal of a firearm certificate, he may surrender his current shotgun certificate and apply for a new one to take effect on the same day as the firearm certificate, such certificates being referred to as being co-terminus. In the latter case, a reduced fee will be paid for the shotgun certificate.

Transfer and Sale of Shotguns

'Transfer' means sale, letting or hire, giving as a gift or lending for a period of more than 72 hours. These do not apply where the person acquiring the gun is a registered firearms dealer, or someone exempt from the need to hold a certificate.

When both parties to the transfer hold certificates, the following requirements apply:

1. A person transferring a shotgun must enter details of the gun on to the new holders' certificate. Within seven days of the transaction he must also send a notice of the transaction to the chief officer of police who granted his shotgun certificate. (Please note that the police who granted the certificate might not be the local police force). If the person transferring the shotgun is exempt from the need to hold a certificate, he should notify details of the transaction to the chief officer of police who granted the certificate of the gun's new holder.

2. A person who acquires a shotgun must send a note of the transaction within 7 days of the transaction taking place to the chief officer of police who granted his certificate.

The notice sent to the chief officer of police must contain a description of the shotgun (including any identification number) and the nature of any transaction and the name and address of the other person involved in the transaction. Any change of address by the certificate holder must be notified to the police without undue delay.

Visitors to Great Britain

Visitors wishing to bring a shotgun or firearm into Great Britain, to possess one here, or to purchase a shotgun for personal use here, need to obtain a visitor's firearm or shotgun permit.

You will need a permit if you are not resident in Great Britain and wish to:

1. Bring a firearm or shotgun into Great Britain for use on a private estate for sport or to take part in a shooting competition or event.

2. Buy a shotgun in Great Britain for use here, or to take home with you.

3. Use a shotgun which you own in Great Britain, and have lodged here with a registered firearms dealer.

An application for a permit must be made on your behalf by a sponsor, resident in Great Britain, to the chief officer of police for the area in which the sponsor lives. Application forms are available on-line on most police websites.

If you are thinking of sponsoring a visitor to Great Britain and require further guidance, first you should contact your local police firearms department.

If you are a member of a shooting association, contact its Firearms Team or legal advisor.

10

SHOOTING AGENTS

Shooting in the British Isles

Shooting agents let various forms of shooting in a variety of ways. Days can be bought singly by individuals or by groups for one or more days. Shooting agents do not usually find places for individuals wishing to join a syndicate on a permanent basis, although it may be worth asking. Membership of a syndicate is usually through advertisements in shooting periodicals or by word of mouth.

Agents advertise regularly in all the country and shooting-oriented magazines. In addition, many of the top estate agents maintain departments specializing in the letting of shooting.

Shooting Abroad

These days there are wonderful opportunities to shoot abroad, whether it is partridge in Spain, pheasants in Hungary (beware, since some of the shooting is very commercialised and not very sporting), quail in Florida or duck and geese in Canada.

There are agents who specialise in organising these events, which is just as well, since shooting abroad can be fraught with pitfalls.

Each country has its own laws with regard to such details as: the movement of firearms into and out of the destination country; game licences; shotgun and firearm certificate requirements and the carriage and purchase of ammunition – for example, India allows only 50 cartridges to be brought in by one person and

Indian-made ammunition is expensive and different in quality to that available at home.

It is not practicable to tabulate the legal requirements that must be satisfied for other countries since changes occur so frequently. Anyone wishing to shoot abroad should use the services and expertise of a shooting agent.

Those confident enough to organise their own trips are still advised to seek advice from the relevant embassy or consulate. Even then, it is advisable to seek further information from a helpful agent who might be aware of problems that will not necessarily be mentioned by the embassy staff.

11

GAMESHOOTING SEASONS

There are a number of gamebirds, waterfowl (ducks, geese and waders) and other bird species, as well as mammals, which can be shot legally. For many there is a close season when it is illegal to shoot them, and this helps to ensure that they are able to breed successfully and move between breeding and wintering grounds. The bird quarry species and their open seasons in England, Wales, Scotland, Northern Ireland, the Isle of Man and the Channel Islands are shown opposite with notes below.

NOTES TO TABLE OPPOSITE

High water mark

England and Wales: The area of sea shore which is more often than not covered by the flux and reflux of the four ordinary tides occurring midway between springs and neaps.

Scotland: Area between high and low water marks of ordinary spring tides

Northern Ireland: The limit of where the living seaweed is attached to the stones of the foreshore.

Isle of Man

* Currently a voluntary ban on shooting red grouse is in place.

** Geese can only be shot under general licence under the Wildlife Act 1990.

See the Department of Agriculture Fisheries and Forestry (DAFF) website for terms and conditions of general licences

GAMEBIRD AND WATERFOWL
OPEN SEASONS (dates inclusive)

Species	England & Wales	Scotland	Northern Ireland	Isle of Man
Pheasant	Oct 1–Feb 1	Oct 1–Feb 1	Oct 1–Jan 31	Oct 1–Jan 31
Grey Partridge	Sep 1–Feb 1	Sep 1–Feb 1	Sep 1–Jan 31	Protected (ban in force)
Red-legged Partridge	Sep 1–Feb 1	Sep 1–Feb 1	Sep 1- Jan 31	Sep 13–Jan 31
Red Grouse	Aug 12–Dec 10	Aug 12–Dec 10	Aug 12–Nov 30	Aug 25–Oct 31 *
Black Grouse	Aug 20-Dec 10 (Somerset, Devon and New Forest: Sep 1–Dec 10)	Aug 20–Dec 10	–	–
Ptarmigan	–	Aug 12–Dec 10	–	–
Duck & Goose (inland)	Sep 1–Jan 31	Sep 1–Jan 31	Sep 1–Jan 31	Ducks Sep 1–Jan 31 Geese** July 1–Mar 31
Duck & Goose (below High Water Mark) – see page 120	Sep 1–Feb 20	Sep 1–Feb 20	Sep 1–Jan 31	Ducks Sep 1–Jan 31 Geese ** Jul 1–Mar 31
Common Snipe	Aug 12–Jan 31	Aug 12–Jan 31	Sep 1–Jan 31	Sep 1–Jan 31
Jack Snipe	Protected	Protected	Sep 1–Jan 31	Protected
Woodcock	Oct 1–Jan 31	Sep 1–Jan 31	Oct 1–Jan 31	Oct 1–Jan 31
Golden Plover	Sep 1–Jan 31	Sep 1–Jan 31	Sep 1–Jan 31	Protected
Coot/Moorhen	Sep 1–Jan 31	Sep 1–Jan 31	Protected	Protected

SHOOTING IN THE CHANNEL ISLANDS

Guernsey

1. The close season for game (rabbit only) runs from Mar 1 until Sept 30 inclusive. Owners/occupiers of land can kill game on their land at any time of year. Additionally, any person who has, in their possession, written permission from the owner/occupier of land may hunt or kill rabbits on that land at any time of year.

(Island of Guernsey, Ordinance of the States XXXII 1994 – The Protection of Game Ordinance 1994)

2. The open season for birds (pheasant, partridge, snipe, woodcock and collared dove) runs from Oct 1 to Jan 31.

3. Woodpigeon may be taken at any time under The Protection of Wild Birds Ordinance 1949.

Jersey

1. In Jersey there are no game seasons and gamebirds can only be shot under licence for the protection of agriculture. All wild birds are protected with the exception of carrion crow, magpie, feral pigeon and woodpigeon which may be shot under licence. However the Minister for Planning and Environment may license any person to do anything which would otherwise constitute an offence against wildlife.

(Conservation of Wildlife (Jersey) Law 2000 Article 16(1) as amended)

2. In Jersey it is illegal to release or allow to escape into the wild any pheasant, red-legged partridge or grey partridge except under licence.

(Conservation of Wildlife (Jersey) Law 2000 Article 15(1)(b) and (3))

WATERFOWL SPECIES WHICH CAN BE SHOT

England, Wales & Scotland

The species that can be shot during their open season are:

(Wildlife and Countryside Act 1981)

Duck	Gadwall, Goldeneye, Mallard, Pintail, Pochard Shoveler, Teal, Tufted duck, Wigeon
Goose	Canada* , Greylag , Pink-footed, White-fronted** (England and Wales only)
Wader	Golden plover, Common snipe, Woodcock
Other	Coot, Moorhen

*Canada geese

This species can be shot throughout the year (i.e. during the close season) in England, Wales and Scotland only under the terms and conditions of specific general licences.

**White-fronted geese

There are two races: European white-fronted goose, which can be shot throughout England and Wales, and the Greenland white-fronted goose, wintering mainly on the west coast of Wales. The latter is part of a declining population which is expected shortly to receive full statutory protection but, in the meantime, continues to be subject to a voluntary no-shooting moratorium by BASC-affiliated clubs.

Northern Ireland

The species that can be shot during their open season are:
(Wildlife (Northern Ireland) Order 1985)

Duck Gadwall, Goldeneye, Mallard, Pintail, Pochard, Ruddy Duck, Scaup, Shoveler, Teal, Tufted Duck, Wigeon

Goose Canada, Greylag, Pink-footed

Wader Common snipe, Jack snipe, Golden plover, Woodcock

Isle of Man

The following species can be shot during the open season:
(Wildlife Act 1990)

Duck Mallard, Teal, Wigeon

Goose * Canada, Greylag

Wader Common snipe, Woodcock

* The geese listed can only be shot during the open season as specified on the general licence. See the DAFF website.

Guernsey and Jersey

The shooting of ducks and geese is not permitted.

For information on the use of non-lead shot for waterfowl please see specific technical information from BASC Research Team or Country Offices.

GROUND GAME OPEN SEASONS
(dates inclusive)

Species	England & Wales	Scotland	Northern Ireland	Isle of Man
Brown Hare	Jan 1–Dec 31 Moorland & unenclosed land is subject to a close season (see below)	Open Season Oct 1–Jan 31	Aug 12–Jan 31*	Brown or common hare Oct 1–Jan 31
Mountain Hare		Open season Aug 1–Feb 28/29		
Rabbit	Jan 1–Dec 31 Moorland & unenclosed land is subject to a close season (see below)	Jan 1–Dec 31 Moorland & unenclosed land is subject to a close season (see below)	Rabbit is classed as a pest and therefore not subject to a close season	No close season

* The Special Protection Order previously issued to give **Irish hare** additional protection is no longer in place and therefore the Irish Hare is now subject to an open season as above.

Moorland and unenclosed land does not include arable land or detached portions of land less than 25 acres which adjoin arable land.

In **England** and **Wales** occupiers or authorised persons may only take and kill ground game on moorland or unenclosed land between 1 September and 31 March inclusive. Firearms may only be used for such purposes between 11 December and 31 March.

(Ground Game Act 1880 Section 1 (3) and Ground Game (Amendment) Act 1906 Section 2)

In **Scotland**, the occupier of the land or persons authorised by him may kill rabbit throughout the year on moorland and unenclosed land (not being arable) by all legal means other than by shooting, and by means of firearms over the period from 1 July to 31 March inclusive. Hares are subject to a close season (see table previous page).

SUNDAY AND CHRISTMAS DAY SHOOTING

England and Wales

No game may be killed or taken in any county on Sunday or Christmas Day. Game for the purposes of this section means pheasant, partridge, red grouse, black grouse and hare.

Orders prohibiting the shooting of wildfowl on Sundays made under sections 2 and 13 of the Protection of Birds Act 1954 still in existence are in the following counties: Anglesey, Brecknock, Caernarvon, Carmarthen, Cardigan, Cornwall, Denbigh, Devon, Doncaster, Glamorgan, Great Yarmouth County Borough, Isle of Ely, Leeds County Borough, Merioneth, Norfolk, Pembroke, Somerset, North and West Ridings of Yorkshire.

Scotland

There are no statutory restrictions on the killing of game on Sunday or Christmas Day but it is not customary to do so. The wildfowl species listed may not be shot on Sunday or Christmas Day.

Northern Ireland

It is an offence to kill any wild bird, gamebird or hare on a Sunday. Although there is no restriction on killing any wild bird, gamebird or hare on Christmas Day, provided it does not fall on a Sunday, it is not customary to do so. There is no prohibition on shooting deer on any day during the open season.

Isle of Man

The killing or taking of game is not permitted on Sunday. There are no restrictions on shooting on Christmas Day unless it falls on a Sunday.

Guernsey

Shooting is not permitted on Sunday or Christmas Day.

Jersey

The use of a firearm to kill any wild bird or animal is not permitted on Sunday, Good Friday and Christmas Day unless acting under and in accordance with the terms or conditions of a licence.

NIGHT SHOOTING

Night is defined as between one hour after sunset until one hour before sunrise (except Jersey – *see below*).

England, Wales and Scotland
The shooting of game at night is not permitted. Ground game (rabbit and hare – which is subject to a close season in Scotland) may be shot at night by an occupier of land or one other person authorised by the occupier, with the permission of the holder of the shooting rights under Wildlife and Countryside Act 1981 Schedule 7, unless the occupier has the exclusive rights.

Northern Ireland
Night shooting of any wild bird, gamebird, hare or deer is prohibited. Foxes and rabbits may be shot (lamped) at night.

Isle of Man
Night shooting of rabbits is permitted by the use of suppressed firearms or sound moderated shot guns, lamps and dogs. Night shooting of any game, bird or vermin is not permitted under the Game Act 1927.

Guernsey
Night shooting is not permitted.

Jersey
The use of a firearm to kill any wild bird or animal is not permitted between sunset and sunrise on any day unless acting under and in accordance with the terms or conditions of a licence.

See the BASC website for full details.

12

THE REST OF THE TEAM

Some people naturally like to know what happens behind the scenes and those who aren't interested probably miss out on a great deal. They might turn up to a shoot and leave at the end, none the wiser as to how the day had been organised and orchestrated. A well-organised driven day's shooting involves a great deal of organisation and potentially a team of supporters which far outnumbers the Guns. We all like to think that we matter in some way; and keepers, beaters, pickers-up and other shoot supporters need to feel appreciated or, like anybody else taken for granted, they may perform indifferently at best, diabolically at worst. If Guns take a genuine interest in the back-up team, they will be rewarded with better sport. In a well-organised shoot, the Guns are but one part of a team.

THE GAMEKEEPER

Some shoots operate on a self-help basis without a keeper but this section is concerned only with keepered shoots. Whether the keeper is full-time or part-time employed, he (or she) is the lynchpin of a shoot. Few people realise just how much keepers do, often with little or no assistance. The following are some of the major tasks of a keeper.

Managing the Habitat

Throughout the year there are jobs to be done and these have to tie in with natural cycles and the weather. Cover crops are planted each spring but woodland cover can only be cut down after the nesting seasons, while planting and most other tree work is confined to the winter and on the moors there is a statutory season for heather burning.

Opportunities for holidays are severely restricted at any time of the year.

Predator Control

In view of the constant threats from predators, it is sometimes surprising that so many game birds survive to maturity, but it is the responsibility of the keeper to see that they do.

Ground predators such as foxes, stoats, weasels, mink and rats can wreak havoc in no time at all and their ability to outwit man is awe-inspiring.

Winged predators, particularly crows and magpies, plunder nests and are a generally harmful influence on the well-being of game birds. The keeper has a variety of means of control at his disposal. For crows he can deploy Larsen traps while for mammals he can use a variety of other traps or set snares. These must be operated in accordance with sometimes complex laws and generally require daily inspection. A keeper can also attempt to shoot predators. All these methods are time-consuming but best done at dawn and dusk. Shooting is actually a fairly inefficient method when trying to control ground pests.

It may seem that a keeper's life is ruled by routine - feeding the poults, visiting the trap line, the seasonal cycle of jobs - but it is far from a nine-to-five existence. Weather and local conditions often dictate the day's work, the unexpected frequently occurs and the keeper is always on-call.

There are human as well as animal predators and all keepers face the threat of poaching. The romantic view of the poacher as a harmless rustic simply stealing for the pot is certainly not true now, and even in the past there were many bloody encounters between keepers and gangs of ruffians operating on a grand scale. With shot birds fetching under a pound from a game dealer today there is little attraction in taking mature birds so criminal activity today is often on an industrial scale with release pens being raided to take large numbers of birds stolen for resale. Without police assistance, it will be a brave, or foolhardy, keeper who intervenes. Similarly, illegal hare coursing or deer poaching involves characters whom it would be unwise to challenge alone.

Rearing Game

Rearing game, notably pheasants, partridge and duck, is a much more predictable business these days and much less vulnerable to the vagaries of nature than it used to be when keepers relied on rearing from eggs taken from their own surviving game stocks. Nevertheless the keeper has to know what he is doing. Fewer and fewer keepers rear game from eggs, instead they buy in poults. These have to be protected from predators and extremes of weather, but due to the skills of the keeper, the losses are kept to a minimum. Once released, reared game needs to be fed and watered, a job much alleviated by automatic feeders and drinkers.

Preparing for a Shoot

In consultation with the shoot host or captain, the keeper may well have to choose the drives and place the pegs for the guns for each drive. He must recruit beaters and ensure there are sufficient pickers-up. Regardless of the precise division of responsibilities, there has to be close coordination between host and keeper so that each knows exactly which drives are to be shot, in which order and in which way depending on the wind direction, plus any other idiosyncrasies relevant to the day.

A Shooting Day

The keeper has little chance to relax on a shooting day until he finally reaches home in the evening. Quite apart from normal routine chores at home, he must arrive at the rendez-vous for the Guns well in advance. He is not so much concerned with the Guns – that is the host's responsibility – as with marshalling his own force of beaters and other helpers. Throughout the day the keeper(s) must carefully direct the beaters to be as efficient as possible. If the beating team is inexperienced it will require extra attention if it is to be effective.

Very often, due to the weather or possibly the whim of the host, it may be necessary to change or adjust the plan for the day. The keeper needs to be flexible and able to accommodate sudden changes of plan calmly and without fuss. At the end of the shoot, the keeper will lay out the bag and, assuming there are enough birds to go round, will give each Gun a brace of birds. This is the moment when the Guns show their appreciation by shaking hands with the keeper, at the same time discreetly slipping a tip into his palm.

Once the Guns have dispersed, the host may wish to discuss the day with the keeper. But the keeper's day is still far from over. He has the shot game to consider which must be handled correctly to enter the food chain. Then there is a host of other jobs, from feeding his dogs to topping up feeders and perhaps even patrolling at night for unwanted visitors.

The keeper will then have to deal with any surplus game, complying with all the strict food safety standards. Selling game helps offset the costs of running the shoot, albeit in a small way. Much British game is sold to the Continent by game dealers.

Beaters

A driven shoot is one where the game is pushed or driven towards the Guns by a team of beaters. Usually, the beaters will be controlled and directed by the keeper. He knows where the birds are and where he wants them to be driven to. Beaters must be told exactly what is required of them in order to be most effective. Many shoots are fortunate in having regular beaters who know the ground, an absolutely essential pre-requisite, and who know intuitively what their job is.

Nevertheless, however experienced the beating team, it needs to be led competently and must be disciplined. Beating needs to be conducted with purpose. It should not be treated as an opportunity for a monumental chin-wag between the participants. The beaters must move through cover methodically, carefully exploring any potential places of concealment that might contain birds.

Dogs

Some keepers will allow beaters to be accompanied by good, conscientious dogs but they must ensure their dogs behave with a high degree of discipline. Dogs which rampage through cover, chasing birds and flushing them wildly are a menace. Indeed, if asked to beat and to bring a dog, it is extremely rude to bring a dog which does not have a clue what it is supposed to do. Like its owner, the dog must have a well-directed sense of purpose. The key advantages of dogs are that they can reach into undergrowth which is impenetrable to humans and can cover a great deal more ground than humans. This is particularly useful when beating through crops where birds enjoy total overhead cover.

Discipline

It is certainly not a hard-and-fast indicator, but there does seem to be a connection between the amount of noise made by the beaters and the quality of a shoot. On a good and well-keepered shoot, experienced beaters will probably make very little noise, which really must be kept to a minimum if the birds are not to be jittered into flushing too early.

Beating on a grouse moor requires just as much discipline as in a pheasant covert; if anything, the grouse moor demands even more rigid discipline from the beaters. At least on a moor, the only cover is heather and that should not be higher than knee level at its highest; indeed, anything over 12" is hard work for beaters and dogs and, more significantly, for grouse. Grouse are truly wild birds and therefore acutely alert to danger. Thus beaters have to keep carefully in line.

On a pheasant shoot, beaters are armed with sticks with which to beat undergrowth whereas on the grouse moor, beaters will carry shorter sticks with a flag attached to it. These days, almost invariably, the flag will be a large square cut from a plastic fertiliser sack, useful because of the penetrating, cracking noise it makes when flapped about. The noise and visual effect of the flag's movement helps to dissuade birds from flying back through the beating line. Good beaters will also know when to wave their flags vigorously, notably if a bird is trying to fly along the beating line or away from the gun line. There should never be a need to make any other noise, especially not verbally.

Stops

In addition to the walking beaters, some drives may necessitate the deployment of a stop or maybe several stops. Stops' primary function is to stand at likely escape points which birds may try to use, usually either side of the beating line, and maybe remain static for much or all of a drive. The stop's aim is to act as a deterrent to birds trying to exit at the sides of the drive and not over the guns. Sometimes, a Gun may be asked to act as a stop, with the purpose of shooting any game flying out of the sides.

Experienced beaters will know what to wear. Beating can be cruel to clothing which, therefore, should be robust, appropriate to the weather conditions and, above all, blend in with the surroundings.

Pickers-up

Pickers-up have trained dogs to retrieve shot game on driven shoots. They will usually stand at some distance behind the Gun, or Guns, so that they can mark any shot birds. Dead birds will normally be left to the end of the drive, but a dog should be sent immediately to retrieve any wounded birds or runners, as a well-trained dog retrieving game will not disturb the shooting. It is important to show respect for the quarry by humanely dispatching wounded birds as quickly as possible and ensuring that shot game is not wasted.

Guns should make a point of acknowledging the presence of pickers-up at the start of every drive and ensuring the pickers-up acknowledge them too.

The Gun and the picker-up should also confer at the end of the drive to make sure that all the birds are picked.

Position of Pickers-up

Pickers-up should be placed behind the Guns in order to pick wounded or dead birds.

Pickers-up should aim to position themselves behind those Guns that do not have their own dogs. Should they be behind a Gun with a dog, they should always ask the Gun, usually at the end of the drive but not necessarily so, if that Gun would prefer to allow his or her own dog to pick the birds within the immediate vicinity of the peg or butt. Where picking-up can become disturbing is when pickers-up do not consult the Guns and just pick everything in sight.

If the opportunity arises, it can benefit the Gun enormously to see a shoot from another perspective by volunteering to beat or pick-up. It is well worth the experience.

13

HOW TO SHOOT

Introduction

This chapter has been left towards the end quite deliberately because it is both pointless and irresponsible to go shooting unless one knows what one is doing. It is pointless, also, to shoot if one has no respect or interest in the quarry, not least wanting to eat it subsequently. Thus, reading this chapter first or, even worse, only reading this chapter, will inevitably result in disaster for the absolute beginner. Hopefully, this is not the case. The point is that the actual act of shooting is but one small facet of a day's shooting: while it may be a significant element for the gameshooter, there is a great deal involved in a day's shooting which should be apparent having read the previous 12 chapters. It should be noted that the advice here is limited and in no way can be considered a sensible or realistic alternative to attending lessons with a qualified shooting coach.

Essential Preparation

Most of the advice which follows has been mentioned already in previous chapters but it is particularly relevant to ensure that the gameshooter is as ready as possible to shoot. Prior to taking a stand at the beginning of a day's shooting, the gameshooter can do several things to reduce his or her chances of missing the quarry.

Gun Fitment and Familiarisation

The gun must fit. As already stated, too much length in the stock can have a dramatically disastrous effect on the firer's marksmanship. Too short or too long a stock will result in an unnatural and uncomfortable posture and therefore poor marksmanship again. Do not worry too much about barrel length as a beginner but try to buy a gun with average-length barrels of 28". In due course you may find that you prefer 30" barrels, which are considered long but maybe better for tackling high birds; alternatively you may opt for short 25" barrels which some prefer when shooting grouse.

Having bought your gun, seek advice from a qualified shooting coach who will be able to help ensure that you end up with a perfectly fitting gun. Familiarise yourself with your gun by devoting time to mounting the empty gun into your shoulder, as often as practicable. More importantly, spend as much time as possible firing at clays.

Clothing and Equipment

This subject has been covered fairly exhaustively already but it cannot be emphasised enough how important it is that your clothing and other equipment is comfortable and, where appropriate, properly adjusted.

Mental Attitude

If you are not in the mood or your mind is on other matters, your performance will almost certainly suffer. You need to be relaxed and at peace with the world to shoot well. It is essential, therefore, to leave plenty of time in which to assemble your equipment and check that you have everything you will need, and then to reach your destination in good time and to enable you to get your bearings once there. To elaborate on this, forgetting an item of equipment can put you off your stride for the whole day. Arriving at the meet with seconds to spare or actually late, particularly after a tense or stressful journey, can be catastrophic for one's peace of mind and subsequent marksmanship.

By arriving early – a quarter of an hour is a good benchmark to aim for – you can achieve several things and, by the appointed hour, be ready to hear your host's brief and then start the day without being guilty of causing a delay while you try belatedly to organise yourself.

A few things you might achieve in advance, include putting on your boots, coat and other apparel and getting comfortable, allowing your dog to stretch its legs, maybe having a cup of coffee, introducing yourself to other guns and the keeper, if he is there, and just generally attuning yourself to your surroundings. Once you have been briefed and arrived at the first stand you should be ready to start shooting with confidence.

Acquiring the Target

At this stage it must be stressed that footwork, or how you stand, is an often ignored but absolutely critical aspect of shooting. Stand with your feet comfortably apart. If shooting off your right shoulder, stand with your left foot forward slightly and vice versa if left-shouldered. This stance gives you a more stable platform than just standing with your feet close together. While waiting for birds, rest your weight on your back foot.

As a bird appears, lock your gaze on to it, transfer your weight to your forward foot and grip your gun with the muzzles up and stock down so that you will be able to raise the gun naturally into your shoulder at the right moment. [Do not mount your gun to your shoulder at this stage. In this way, your muzzles should be pointing in the direction of the bird and aligned with your eyes, which will be locked on to the target.]

As the bird approaches within range, not before, start to mount the gun so that the barrels are behind the bird and then, as the stock comes firmly into your shoulder, swing through the bird, pulling the trigger as you blot out the bird's head and then – and this is absolutely vital – continue to swing through. The action of swinging from behind the bird will result automatically in the gun matching the speed of the bird.

Do not put the gun into your shoulder and wait for the bird to come into range and then try to swing; it simply will not work and you will miss every time.

The author's son's coach taught him the following mantra: '***bum, belly, beak, bang***', which neatly encompasses the route the barrels must take if the target is to be hit. As a final adjunct, failure to keep swinging through after pulling the trigger will always result in a miss behind the bird.

Similarly, do not try and cheat by merely raising your gun and firing in front of the bird without swinging, in the hope that the bird will fly into your shot pattern because it never will unless you are a naturally, phenomenally good shot. This ambushing technique is also known as poking.

Crossing Birds

For a right-handed shot the left-crossing bird is easier to engage than a right-crossing bird because the stock will be pressed into the cheek automatically. Initially your feet will remain apart as already described but if necessary you may have to pivot on the ball of your right foot, simultaneously moving your left foot with the momentum of your swinging upper body.

With a right-crossing bird, you need to consciously marry the stock to your cheek. Although not an inviolable principle, you will be more likely not to lift a foot but rather will pivot on the balls of both feet. It is a good idea to practise mounting your gun on imaginary fast and slow left and right crossers until the process becomes second-nature.

Distance

To avoid the risk of pricking or wounding birds, measure out 40 yards on the ground and try to fix the distance in your mind so that with practice you can gauge it instinctively. On a drive you may be able to mark a tree or other feature that will help to establish the limit of your range. In reality, most pheasants will be less than 30 yards high.

The maximum range at which to fire at a bird is 40 yards. It is quite possible to kill birds beyond this range but such shots should be avoided by all but the best shots since there is a greater risk of merely wounding birds.

High Birds

The most important factor with high or distant birds is to swing fast and boldly, consciously adding a lead in front of the bird before pulling the trigger. The higher the bird, the more generous must be the lead. The amount of lead and the technique will be unique to the individual gun and can only be perfected with much practice.

Grouse and Partridge

The techniques described so far give a few pointers applicable to all situations but are mainly relevant to pheasant, high-flying partridge and duck. Grouse and partridge possess similar flight characteristics, although partridge can also fly like pheasant. This section, therefore, refers mainly to grouse.

Grouse are distinguished by great speed, manoeuvrability and the fact that they generally fly very low. This last factor dictates a significant acceleration of the techniques described already. Whereas shooting at low pheasants is to be strongly discouraged, grouse usually offer no alternative.

It is essential that the novice is coached and supervised if he has never shot grouse before. Indeed, to cut one's teeth on grouse, never having shot pheasant, should not happen because the margins for safety when shooting driven grouse are vastly narrower than those appertaining to pheasant. Pheasant shooting, by and large, is almost leisurely compared to the urgency and split-second reactions called for when shooting driven grouse.

The gameshooter does not have the freedom to swing widely because he must avoid swinging through the line or inevitably he will point his gun at his neighbour and could easily shoot him or her. The process of acquiring and hitting grouse is little different to that for slower species, however everything happens that much more quickly and there could be many closely packed potential targets approaching simultaneously.

The gun must discipline himself not to fire randomly into a covey but to select a bird and concentrate solely on that bird until he pulls the trigger. If he leaves it too late he will have to interrupt his swing to avoid pointing at his neighbour and then attempt to re-acquire the target behind the gun line.

Having advised the reader to avoid taking birds over 40 yards away, with a grouse approaching head-on it is necessary to pick your target early when the bird could be maybe 80 yards away. By the time the trigger has been pulled the same bird could probably be less than 40 yards away and, if killed, could land close to the firer's butt.

14

ROUGH SHOOTING

Introduction

Rough shooting is great fun and can be immensely rewarding and satisfying. It is the nearest to true hunter-gathering that the gameshooter can aspire to, as he or she walks up ground in search of quarry, be it game or vermin. Fundamentally, it is about shooting for the pot, hence another term for rough shooting is 'pottering'. Any number of people can participate but the norm is to involve maybe only two or three Guns. Dogs are a vital component, both to find and flush quarry and, subsequently, to retrieve it.

Rough shooting is far removed from the discipline and structure of driven gameshooting but be under no illusion because it is potentially the most hazardous form of gameshooting. As such, it is essential that the uninitiated be accompanied by an experienced rough shooter. Why is it hazardous?

Principally, it is likely to take place through woods or over rough, uneven terrain punctuated with parcels of rough cover and hedgerows. The nature of the ground often will cause Guns to be out of sight, although not out of range, of each other. In such circumstances, the carelessly considered shot at a low bird in or entering cover could prove fatal to the target but also to a dog and more critically, to a neighbouring Gun. As an aside, while ground game may be the main quarry on a rough shoot, the participants would be sensible to forbid shooting ground game except in clear, open country.

Rough shooting is not an undertaking for the faint-hearted and participants need to be fit.

Technique

Unlike driven shooting which requires varying degrees of elaborate planning by the participants, rough shooting is more spontaneous but still should not be treated too casually. You need to know the boundaries of the land you are shooting over to avoid the embarrassment of being caught trespassing, which, *in extremis*, could end up with a court appearance. You need to plan your route beforehand, taking into account the wind direction so that as much as possible of your route is into the wind. This will improve your chances of getting nearer your quarry. If you approach from upwind, your quarry is more likely to become aware of your presence and take off out of range.

Participants should strive to be visible to each other as much as possible to reduce the risk of accidents. They should refrain from chatting too much, indeed they should attempt to be as quiet as possible. When controlling your dog – or trying to – use a whistle, which will be less intrusive than an ever-rising vocal cacophony.

Dogs should be allowed to work and quarter the ground but in a controlled fashion so that they are not too far in front of the Guns. If they are allowed to stray too far out in front, they are useless since they will disturb game out of range of the Guns and, almost invariably, the game will fly in any direction except over the Guns.

Despite its informal nature, rough shooting still requires a high degree of discipline on the part of the Guns. Each must be aware of all participants' whereabouts at all times. Also, they must scan likely target areas for other people, especially if shooting near a public road, footpath or bridleway. Is there a dog-walker behind that hedge? Is there a rambler behind that wall?

Walked-up birds are much less likely to fly high, offering a silhouette against a clear sky. Instead, they might fly low and level at head height, presenting their tails to the Guns. Indeed, it is one of the inevitabilities of rough shooting that the majority of shots could be at going-away birds. Shooting birds up their tail end is far less satisfying than shooting a sporting bird out front cleanly in the head. If a bird gets up near to you, try to pause before you shoot since you risk rendering a bird unusable if it is shot too close. Do not shoot for the sake of shooting.

Equipment

The Guns' intention should be to travel as lightly as practicable, avoiding festooning themselves with totally unnecessary paraphernalia. Do you really need to carry a *gamebag* over your shoulder? Quite possibly you do but a *shooting coat* with big pockets may have room for a couple of pheasants. Any piece of equipment with a shoulder strap such as a cartridge bag and gun sleeve may be a hindrance to gun mounting.

Alternatively, it may be feasible to cache anything that has been shot at certain points on your route, to await collection at the end of your foray. A full *cartridge belt* is essential but do you need more? If so, stuff a couple of handfuls of *loose cartridges* in your coat pocket. Try to avoid carrying a *cartridge bag*, however small, as it will be a hindrance. Leave your *gunsleeve* in your car. A *stick* will also be a hindrance. Dress according to the weather.Do bear in mind that rough shooting can be quite energetic so you may not need to dress as warmly as for a driven shoot. ***Ear defenders*** are essential, as they are in whatever circumstances you may be firing a gun. Carry a ***knife***. Even if the going may be boggy in places, can you get away with not wearing ***waterproof trousers*** – after all it is more weight to haul about? Do not forget your ***whistle*** for the dog. Finally, do carry a ***mobile phone*** as an expedient form of radio to coordinate the shoot as you go along.

Conclusion

Rough shooting epitomises the true spirit of gameshooting. It is not about big bags, as already mentioned, it is about shooting for the pot. To use a Yorkshire maxim 'you only need an ample sufficiency', which in a gameshooting context, means do not shoot more game than you can put to good use either at home in the kitchen or by giving some to somebody else who appreciates the virtues of game.

APPENDIX 1

GLOSSARY OF SHOOTING TERMS

There is little more disheartening for a novice, who is trying to conceal that fact, than hearing his peers using incomprehensible terms. Equally, the sensible novice refrains from over-use of jargon if he is not to stand out as a novice. He should let on that he is a beginner, on the basis that such an admission should result in people offering help and advice; it also warns them to be wary of the actions of a novice. To pretend to be experienced when the opposite is the case is to invite ridicule at best and disgrace in the event of a mistake.

The following list is not all-embracing, but should go a long way towards helping the novice to understand what people are talking about in the shooting field.

The Action contains the gun's firing mechanism; joins the stock to the barrels.

Automatic or more accurately, a semi-automatic. A repeating shotgun which automatically ejects a fired cartridge and places a fresh round into the breech. Held on a shotgun licence, it must not have a magazine capable of holding more than two cartridges. For a greater capacity, a section 1 FAC is required and there are restrictions on quarry that may be shot. Semi-autos are never used on formal shoots but are popular with wildfowlers and pest controllers.

Bag. The total number of birds and ground game shot during the day.

Balled Shot. When pellets fuse to make one shot. Rare and almost invariably destroys the target. Sometimes used as an excuse (a threadbare one) by greedy shots who have destroyed a bird too close to the end of their barrels.

Beater. A person who beats the undergrowth as part of the process of driving game towards the Guns. May be hired, sometimes friends and/or family, sometimes local enthusiasts and frequently a combination of all three.

Bend. The distance between the uppermost edge of the shotgun stock (the comb) and the continuation of a line from the muzzle to the breech of a gun.

Blacking/Blueing. The blue coloration applied to protect gun barrels and, to an extent, reduce shine. Often, actions are blued too.

Bore (or Gauge). In simple terms, the nominal internal diameter of a gun barrel. Occasionally, you may hear the phrase 'checking the bore', which means checking inside the barrels for obstructions. Also a person who bangs on interminably about shooting to the exclusion of anything else.

Box-Lock. A simple, robust action; often recognizable by its squared appearance where it joins the stock.

Brace. A pair. Grouse bags, for example, are tallied in braces, e.g. 102½ brace is 205 head. Partridge are tallied in pairs as should be pheasant, except that, almost always these days, they are tallied in braces.

Broken Gun. Where the barrels are dropped open and clear of the action, exposing the chambers to view.

Bullet. A shaped lead projectile attached (usually) to a brass case containing explosive propellant. Fired from a rifle or handgun.

Butt. The rear or shoulder end of the gun's stock. Also, a butt on a grouse moor is an open shelter provided for each Gun; its purpose being not so much protection as concealment from the quarry.

Cartridge. Rifle, pistol or shotgun ammunition. Never mix different calibres in the same container, e.g. 12 bore and 20 bore, or a smaller cartridge may block the barrel ahead of a larger one and cause the gun to burst – this is not a rare occurrence.

Cartridge Bag. A waterproof leather or canvas bag. The most common type is a capacious container with cutaway, flap and leather/webbing shoulder strap. They are available in 50, 75 and 100-cartridge sizes; 100 cartridges are not light. A good leather one will last more than a lifetime. For shotgun ammunition only.

Cartridge Base. The metal base of the cartridge in the centre of which is the primer. When struck by the firing pin, or striker, the primer ignites the main charge of the cartridge, thereby propelling the shot down the barrel. Some modern cartridges are a one-piece plastic moulding with a primer in the base.

Cartridge Belt. A looped belt which usually carries 25 cartridges (the standard quantity in a box). The closed loop system is probably the best since it prevents cartridges slipping through, as can occur with open loops.

Cast. The gentle bend in the stock from the centre line of the barrels to allow for vagaries of eyesight and physique. 'Cast-off' is to the right, 'Cast-on' is to the left.

Chamber. Where the cartridge is placed in the barrel prior to firing. Make sure your cartridges can be used safely in your gun's chambers. Chamber length and service pressure is usually marked on the flat underside at the chamber end of the barrels.

Choke. The degree of narrowing of the bore at the muzzle end of the barrel. Most shotguns have less choke in the first barrel than the second. The purpose of choke is to concentrate the shot into a smaller area. This does not extend the range but may reduce wounding.

Cocks-Only Day. A day when you do not shoot hen pheasants. A practice usually confined to post-Christmas days and not necessarily on all shoots. Hosts will brief.

Covert. A plantation or small wood offering shelter to birds. The 't' is silent.

Covey. A family of grouse or partridge flying together – usually low and very fast. A very large group of several grouse coveys is known as a pack.

Damascus Barrels. A nineteenth-century method used to make the best shotgun barrels, now superseded. Damascus barrels may be recognised by the attractive and intricate scrolled patterns which are the result of several pieces of steel being twisted together, fused and drilled.

Decoy. An imitation bird which is placed in an advantageous position to lure live birds – either pigeon or duck – over the Guns.

Draw. On most shoots, Guns draw numbers for their first stand or peg. Thereafter, they move up or down usually two places each drive. For the draw, a host might use a pack of cards or purpose-made pegs. Not all hosts bother with a draw, preferring to place individuals for each drive; in such circumstances, some hosts find the urge to place themselves to best advantage irresistible.

Drive. A day will be divided into a number of drives (six or eight on average). After each drive, Guns move a pre-arranged number of pegs for the next drive. Most shoots usually number from the right and move two places numerically after each drive.

Driven Game. Game driven towards standing Guns by beaters.

Ejector. The mechanism on shotguns by which spent cartridge cases are ejected automatically from the gun when it is opened after firing.

Flighting. The means by which wildfowl are shot along flight lines, either on inland pools or on coastal marshes and mudflats at dawn or dusk.

Flush. To make game break cover and fly over the Guns. A flush can also refer to several birds flushed in a pack; which process keepers try to avoid.

Fouling. The deposits left in the barrel after firing, which with corrosive caps will cause pitting if not cleaned out immediately after use.

Game. Within the meaning of the Game Act 1831, the following quarry species are game: pheasant, partridge, grouse, ptarmigan, blackgame, capercailzie, snipe, woodcock, duck, goose and hare.

Game Book. In which the sportsman records his adventures: where, with whom, the bag, a brief resumé of the day, and any highlights – you should write only what you do not mind others reading!

Game-cart. A trailer or vehicle in which dead game is collected and carried during the day.

Game Dealer. A man who sells game – can be a precarious way of earning a living.

Gapes. A disease found in pheasants and partridges which affects the throat and is highly infectious.

Ground Game. Rabbits and hares. More exotically, also deer, and, on the Continent, such species as mouflon and wild boar.

Gun. In addition to the obvious, a term used for a person shooting. 'Gameshot' or 'Gameshooter' is a term for a person who indulges in gameshooting.

Gun Case. A compartmentalized case, the best being of leather-on-wood construction, others being made from canvas-on-wood or moulded plastic, for transporting and storing a gun. Left in the car while shooting. These days, for fairly short journeys, guns tend to be transported in a gun sleeve.

Gundogs. They find game, flush, and retrieve it when shot. Most breeds will combine at least two of these roles, though each has been bred for a particular job. In gameshooting, a spaniel's strength is in finding and flushing game and facing dense undergrowth; labradors excel at retrieving and tackling water; but many gundogs are capable all-rounders. The exceptions are pointers and setters which are generally confined to working on grouse moors.

Gun sleeve. (also Gun Cover) A canvas, plastic or leather protective sleeve in which to carry a gun throughout the day. Particularly useful between drives, especially if a fair amount of vehicle travel is involved.

Hammer Gun. An obsolescent type of shotgun with outside hammers which usually require manual cocking and rarely have safety catches or ejectors. Not for beginners or serious social shooters but they have their devotees and, in practised hands, can perform well.

Hanging. Feathered game should be hung vertically by the neck for several days, depending on the species and according to personal taste; ground game hung by the hind legs. This is for culinary reasons rather than some quirky, exotic ritual. *See* Chapter 8 for a full description.

Hide. A place of concealment from which to shoot such species as pigeon and wildfowl.

High/Tall Birds. Self-explanatory. One of the most sporting targets is a high pheasant with the wind up its tail. The most frequently missed target, a high bird is one at the extreme range (40 yards plus) of a shotgun.

Hill. Something very steep in Scotland, and the somewhat misleading term for a mountain there. Grouse moors in Scotland are often half-way up very steep mountains, with the after-lunch drive almost invariably involving an excruciatingly taxing climb to the butts.

Hip-flask. A source of comfort, usually containing an alcoholic beverage according to the owner's taste. Examples are: sloe gin, sloe vodka, cherry brandy, whisky, whisky and Drambuie, whisky and ginger. While flasks are useful ice-breakers and means of introducing yourself to strangers, they are becoming less popular, not least because shooting and alcohol make very poor bedfellows.

Keeper. The man without whom you would have no sport, in all likelihood. Short for 'Gamekeeper'.

Lead. Another word for 'forward allowance'. The muzzles should be ahead of the target to a varying degree when pulling the trigger. Also an item owners of ill-disciplined dogs always seem to leave at home.

Lock. The firing mechanism part of the action. *See* Box-lock and Side-lock.

Magazine. A leather case with internal compartments, slightly larger than an attaché case, for the carriage of cartridges. An average capacity is about 250 cartridges. Rarely seen except on formal, two-gun days requiring a lot of cartridges.

Mark. A word for warning a fellow Gun that a bird is approaching him. An alternative, more usual cry is 'Over'. Such cries are usually only necessary when birds are hard to see or likely to pass unnoticed. They are seldom heard on large, formal shoots. Also the term for marking the fall of a bird, for pickers-up.

Non-toxic shot. It is now illegal to use lead shot over wetlands, including the foreshore and inland ponds, throughout the UK. Additionally, in England and Wales it is illegal to shoot ducks and geese with lead. The alternatives referred to as non-toxic shot incluse steel, bismuth and tungsten. In general you should use one size larger than lead, and perhaps two sizes larger for steel which is significantly less dense.

Over-and-Under (O/U). A two-barrelled shotgun with one barrel mounted vertically over the other.

Pattern. The concentration of pellets measured in a circle at a given range (usually 30" at 40 yds).

Peg. *See* Stand.

Pellet. A small lead ball (also tungsten matrix, bismuth, steel or tin) of which a number make up the shot load, found in a cartridge. A 12 bore cartridge loaded with $1^{1}/_{16}$ oz (30g) of No. 6 shot (No. 6) may hold up to 280 pellets.

Picker-up. A person with a trained dog who picks up shot game.

Piece. Scottish for packed lunch. Also old English for a gun, hence fowling piece.

Pitting. Corrosion inside barrels due to the effects of rust and fouling in general. Originated by deposits from all cartridges, but especially from cheaper, imported brands. Invariably the result of inadequate cleaning after shooting.

Poking. Aiming with the gun already mounted in the shoulder, without swinging. An excellent way of preserving game since it rarely results in a kill! It is also considered bad form.

Poult. An immature pheasant or partridge. Usually released into a temporary pen at 6-8 weeks old.

Priest. A small cosh used by fisherman to dispatch fish. Increasingly seen in the shooting field and useful for dispatching birds if room can be found for it in a pocket.

Primer. The insert in the centre of the cartridge base which, when struck by the firing pin, ignites the propellant, thereby propelling the shot from the barrels.

Proof. By law, all guns must be nitro-proof tested and stamped accordingly before they can be sold or offered for sale. This means that the assembled action and barrels have been tested to ensure they can withstand a pressure well in excess of that experienced in normal usage. Modern guns are proved for Nitro (smokeless) powder, but some guns still in circulation have been only Black Powder proved. Never use modern cartridges in such a gun: seek professional advice if in doubt.

Pump Gun. Another form of single-barrelled, repeating shotgun with a magazine in a tube under the barrel. Loading and ejection are achieved by pulling back the sliding fore-end. Pump guns, or pump-action shotguns, are awkward to handle. These guns should not be used for gameshooting but are useful for pest control.

Punt Gun. A large bore gun, almost a small artillery piece, mounted in a punt and used for wildfowling. Such is the recoil, that punt guns are usually fired remotely by lanyard (a cord attached to the trigger).

Recoil. The force with which a gun moves rearwards into the shoulder when fired. Although superfluous if the gun is held correctly, recoil pads are available to help absorb some of the recoil. Recoil can be reduced by using lighter load cartridges.

Rifle. A firearm with a spirally-grooved barrel used for long-range shooting, demanding precise accuracy, which fires single high velocity ammunition/bullets. Used for shooting any game of the size of deer or greater, rabbits and other small vermin.

Right and Left or vice versa, but usually this way, since that is the sequence in which the majority of guns are designed to fire. The definition is: when one bird is killed with the right barrel and another with the left, without reloading or dismounting the gun between shots.

Rough shooting. Rough shooting involves Guns walking the ground with dogs to shoot whatever legal quarry is flushed. Normally undertaken by small groups, it can vary from walking the boundaries of a serious game shoot to a few friends out for rabbits or pigeon on a summer evening.

Runner. Quarry which is wounded and moves away from where it landed or was shot. Runners should not be left without making a determined effort to recover them, unless there are pickers-up nearby who should be informed accordingly of the suspected whereabouts of the runners. Be alert to the risk of disrupting the start of the next drive by being over-fastidious trying to pick a runner – that is the job of the picker-up. Just make sure they know about any possible runners.

Safety Catch. Something of a misnomer since it is a mechanical device which can fail to work. It must always be at safe except when aiming at a target with the intention of shooting at it. There is no other occasion when it should be off. Most shotguns have this as a sliding catch immediately to the rear of the top lever, which is thumb operated. On most guns, breaking the gun returns the catch to the safe position automatically. It is not possible to check the position of the safety catch too often.

Shooting School. A place that every wise gameshot should try to visit before the start of the season each year. A variety of different skills can be honed here.

Shooting Stick. A stick with a handle which tips or opens to form a rudimentary seat and has a guard at the base to prevent it sinking into the ground. Something of an aid to infirmity, it is yet another item to be carried and is very rarely likely to be an essential. Can be useful when awaiting a duck flight, though.

Shotgun. A smooth-bore gun used for shooting game and vermin at relatively short ranges, typically 20-40 yards. The most common size is the 12 bore.

Side-Lock. (Hammerless). A refined version of the hammer gun lock and much more expensive. Unlike the normal, squared-off box-lock, it has an elegant rounded plate which lends itself to intricate engraving. Some game shots hold that a side-lock will last longer than a box-lock. Side-locks are easier to detach and some guns are designed with purpose-built detachable locks to facilitate repair, cleaning and maintenance.

Side-by-Side. A shotgun with two barrels sitting side-by-side and, in Great Britain, the standard gameshooting weapon, although there is a steady increase in use of over-and-unders.

Stand/Peg. The place where a Gun stands during a drive. On smarter shoots, each peg will be marked by a stake with a number on the top. Once placed, Guns should indicate their presence to their flanking or neighbouring Guns and never leave the vicinity of their peg unless specifically instructed to do so (usually by their host), until the end of the drive. To move from one's peg, unless concealed from neighbouring Guns anyway, incurs a very real risk of being shot, simply because you are no longer where your neighbours expect you to be.

Stock. The rearmost piece of wood of a shotgun which fits into the shooter's shoulder. Most usually made of walnut, it is easily broken and very expensive to repair. Ideally it should be fitted to the owner for length, cast and bend since, apart from innate inaccuracy on the part of the firer, this is the single biggest cause of missing the target. Stocks can be altered for length relatively easily and inexpensively. Replacing a stock is hideously expensive whatever make of gun you own.

Stop. A stop can be a beater or Gun placed to deter game from escaping along the ground any other way except over the Guns.

Striker. Correct technical term for a firing pin.

Top Lever. The conventional mechanism for breaking open a shotgun, situated forward of the safety catch.

Various. That part of the bag which is not officially classed as game. Most game books have a 'Various' column.

Vermin. Pests and predators that cause considerable damage to crops and game.

Wadding. The card and fibre plugs or plastic moulding in a cartridge between the pellets and the propellant, which prevents gas from escaping past the pellets when the gun is fired and acts as a piston behind the shot charge.

Walking Gun. Usually a Gun who takes his turn to walk with the beaters to shoot birds flying back or out to a side.

Walking-up. In which Guns, by walking across a piece of land, flush game before them and shoot. Most game is shot to the front. Beaters may also be interspersed with Walking Guns.

Wildfowling. The pursuit of wildfowl in wild places, usually on the foreshore; principal quarry in Great Britain being: mallard, wigeon, teal and goose.

APPENDIX 2

USEFUL ADDRESSES

Voluntary Associations

1. British Association for Shooting and Conservation (BASC)
Marford Mill, Rossett, Wrexham, Clwyd LL12 OHL. Tel: 01244 573000.
Fax: 01244 573001.
E-mail: enquiries@basc.org.uk   Website: www.basc.org.uk

Membership is highly recommended and is relatively cheap. Also provides 3rd party liability insurance up to £10m. Advice and courses on all shooting aspects, dogs, etc. Subscription includes a bi-monthly magazine.

2. Country Land and Business Association (CLA)
16 Belgrave Sq, London SW1X 8PQ. Tel. 0207 235 0511. Fax: 0207 235 4696. E-mail: mail@cla.org.uk Website: www.cla.org.uk

CLA represents owners of rural and agricultural land. Advises on all matters, notably legal and taxation. Organizes the Game Fair.

3. The Countryside Alliance
The Old Town Hall, 367 Kennington Road, London SE11 4PT.
Tel: 0207 840 9200. Fax: 0207 793 8484.
E-mail: info@countryside-alliance.org
Website: www.countryside-alliance.org

Formed from the British Field Sports Society (which represented all fieldsports), the Countryside Business Group and Countryside Movement.

4. The Game and Wildlife Conservation Trust

Burgate Manor, Fordingbridge, Hants SP6 1EF

Tel: 01425 52381. Fax: 01425 655848.

E-mail: info@gwct.org.uk Website: www.gwct.org.uk

Possibly the definitive institute, researching practically every aspect of game research and management as well as building and managing a shoot and courses for keepers.

5. The National Gamekeepers Organisation

PO Box 246, Darlington, Co Durham DL1 9FZ

Tel: 01833 660869. E-mail: info@nationalgamekeepers.org.uk

Website: www.nationalgamekeepers.org.uk

6. National Gundog Association. Tel. 01530 223570

Advice on reputable gundog breeders.

7. British Deer Society

Burgate Manor, Fordingbridge, Hants SP6 1EF

Tel. 01425 655434. Fax: 01425 655433.

E-mail: hq@bds.org.uk Website: www.bds.org.uk

Deer management

Sporting Publications

1. *Shooting Times* – weekly
2. *Shooting Gazette* – monthly
3. *The Field* – monthly, plus summer and Christmas issues
4. *Sporting Gun* – monthly
5. *Shooting Sports* – website
6. *Sporting Rifle* – monthly
7. *Sporting Shooter* – monthly
8. *Scottish Field* – monthly
9. *Shooting & Conservation* (BASC) – bi-monthly
10. *Fieldsports* – bi-monthly

Shooting Schools

Wherever you live, there will almost certainly be a shooting school nearby. A web search should give you a wide choice and you will find many listed at www.goshooting.org.uk

INDEX

About BASC

The British Association for Shooting and Conservation (BASC) is the representative body for country shooting in the UK.

It started over a century ago when wildfowlers, concerned at the loss of habitat and threats to their sport, formed the Wildfowlers' Association of Great Britain and Ireland. That was in 1908. By 1981 it was clear that the association, with more than 50,000 members, represented far more than just wildfowlers and the name was changed to the British Association for Shooting and Conservation.

Today BASC, with 135,000 members, is one of the largest field sports organisations in Europe and provides a powerful voice in the public and political arenas for shooting.

With country offices in Scotland, Wales and Northern Ireland, four regional offices in England and its headquarters at Rossett, the association has more than a hundred staff devoted to protecting and promoting shooting sports.

The full-time firearms, gamekeeping, deer, wildfowling and conservation teams are able to give immediate expert advice to members. In one month alone the firearms team will deal with several hundred calls for help from members needing advice, often through difficulties with firearms licensing authorities.

Meanwhile the media and political teams defend our interests among decision makers and in the corridors of power. BASC provides the secretariat for the All-Party Group on Shooting and Conservation at Westminster, ensuring support across the whole political spectrum and providing a direct channel to both government and opposition. With fully-equipped radio and video studios the association provides instant and authoritative comment to the media.

For members there is also unrivalled insurance cover and a wide range of financial benefits. To find out more you can visit www.basc.org.uk or call the membership hotline on 01244 573030.

GUNS & LICENCES

Shotgun Certificate number:...

Referee:...

Gun type/model:..

Serial number: ....

Gun type/model:..

Serial number: ....

Firearm Certificate number:...

First referee:........................... Second referee:...........................

Gun type/model:..

Serial number: ....

Gun type/model:..

Serial number: ....

INSURANCE DETAILS

Insurance company:..

Policy number:..

Policy details:...

....

GUN SERVICING RECORD

Gun..Date serviced:....................
By whom:..

Gun..Date serviced:....................
By whom:..

Gun..Date serviced:....................
By whom:..

CARTRIDGE SUPPLIERS (name/tel/website)

1. Supplier:..
2. Supplier:..
Mail order cartridges: www.justcartridges.com

USEFUL SHOOTING CONTACTS

Name..
Address...
....
....
......................................Tel...

Name..
Address...
....
....
......................................Tel...

Name..
Address...
....
....
......................................Tel...

Name..
Address...
....
....
......................................Tel...

Name..
Address...
....
....
......................................Tel...

USEFUL SHOOTING CONTACTS

Name..
Address...
....
....
....Tel..

Name..
Address...
....
....
....Tel..

Name..
Address...
....
....
....Tel..

Name..
Address...
....
....
....Tel..

Name..
Address...
....
....
....Tel..

Further shooting books from Merlin Unwin Books

Private Thoughts from a Small Shoot
Laurence Catlow £17.99

That Strange Alchemy
Pheasants, trout and a middle-aged man
Laurence Catlow £17.99

Rough Shooting in Ireland
Douglas Butler £20

Wild Duck and their pursuit
Douglas Butler £20

The Sporting Gun's Bedside Companion
Douglas Butler £15.99

The Black Grouse
Patrick Laurie £20

Geese!
Memoirs of a Wildfowler
Edward Miller £20

The Airgun Hunter's Year
Ian Barnett £20

Advice from a Gamekeeper
John Cowan £20

Vintage Guns for the Modern Shot
Diggory Hadoke £30

The British Boxlock Gun & Rifle
Diggory Hadoke £30

The Shootingman's Bedside Book
BB £18.95

A Countryman's Creel
Conor Farrington £14.99

Full details:

www.merlinunwin.co.uk